BREAD, PEACE AND LIBERTY

J. Kreitmann

University Press of America, Inc.
Lanham • New York • London

Library of Congress Cataloging-in-Publication Data

Kreitmann, J.
(Pain, paix, et liberté. English)
Bread, peace, and liberty / by J. Kreitmann.
p.   cm.
Originally published: Nutley, N.J. : Craig Press, c1980.
Includes bibliographical references.
1. Evangelistic work--Philosophy. 2. War--Religious aspects. 3.
Food supply--Religious aspects--Christianity. 4. Freedom (Theology)
I. Title.
BV3790.K6913   1996   269'.2.01--dc20   95-39551 CIP

ISBN 0-7618-0122-7 (pbk: alk: ppr.)

TABLE OF CONTENTS

Foreword v

The Translator vii

The Author ix

Introduction xi

PART ONE: **BREAD** 1

Chapter 1 **Man's Efforts to Assure Himself of the Vital Minimum** 3

Standpoint of the individual: work, thrift, solidarity, insurance 3

Standpoint of the government 8
A political science which takes into account
man's fundamental aspirations.
Different economic regimes
The regulation of economic activities
The optimum density of the population
Anticipating dangers

Chapter 2 **A Generally Forgotten Food: the Bread of Life** 21

What is this bread? 22

What happens to men and nations who are nourished with the bread of life? 26

PART TWO: **PEACE** 35

Chapter 3 **Analysis of the Reasons for Man's Failure to Establish a Lasting Peace** 37

The responsibility of statesmen. 37
"I loved war too much." (Louis XIV)
Democracy and peace

The influence of religions: 41
ancient paganism, Christianity, Islam
Are modern ideologies more conclusive
to peace than the religions?

The research of sociologists 47
The French Institute of Polemology

The biblical revelation. 47

Chapter 4   **Remedies for Avoiding War** 49

*The peace of the great empires: Babylon,
Egypt, Rome* 49

*Peace by a voluntary constraint of
human nature*. 50
Medieval Christianity, the paradise of
the soviets, the masonic ideal, the
great international organization

*Jesus Christ, the Prince of Peace,
initiator of a new humanity*. 57

PART THREE: LIBERTY. 61

Chapter 5   **The Causes of Servitude** 63

Political causes. 63
Dictatorship, democracy; the weariness of
free men; state religions, Roman Catholic
reaction or atheistic materialism; state
medicine; administrative arbitrariness

Economic causes 72
Feudalism and guilds; the hoarding of riches;

ii

authoritarian economic planning economic
subjection the cement of political oppression

Social causes 75

Chapter 6   **The Conquest of Liberty** 81

Apprenticeship in the techniques of liberty 82

Requirements for the present fight for liberty 85
The secret of exceptional strength of character;
the discernment of the Communists and
the blindness of the Westerners; appeal to the
young States of Asia and Africa

CONCLUSION
The Tragedy of Our World 92

FOREWORD

This book of modest size will interest two groups of readers.

First, there are those who wish to eradicate famine in India and Africa, war in Asia, and totalitarianism everywhere. The author has met all three in Europe. A major of the French artillery, he was captured and put behind Hitler's barbed wire early in World War II.

Since he was not assigned to Stalag 13 under Colonel Klink and Sergeant Schulze, he must have been pretty miserable; but he was fortunate not to have been tortured and killed as many of the majors were. After the war he served the civil government in organizing the food supply and establishing financial credit. M. Kreitmann therefore has an intimate knowledge of Bread, Peace, and Liberty.

Nevertheless, this is not a book of reminiscences. Rather it examines the causes and conditions of war and famine, and suggests methods for coping with them. Famine is a present fact, and wars continue. It is not merely possible, it is likely, and maybe inevitable that Europe and America will again become battlefields. For this reason the author's suggestions as to what to do in such an emergency deserve serious consideration. Further, inflation with its threat of totalitarianism might be diminished if enough people consider the author's views on economics.

In his studies, for M. Kreitmann holds a Doctor of Jurisprudence from the University of Paris, and a diploma from the Free School of Political Science, he has discovered a famine that is not physical, a war that is not military, and a totalitarianism that is worse than political. They are known as the world, the flesh, and the devil.

This brings into view the second group of readers—or at least a sub-group included in the first—who will enjoy this book because they have already discovered the spiritual realities that conquer these enemies. Such readers will be interested from two points of view. The first, and by far the more important, is their desire to present to the public the Bread of Life, the Prince of Peace, and the King of Kings. The second is not without importance, either. It has to do with the method of presentation. In America we are accustomed to huge rallies and well advertised campaigns; and we have exported these tactics to Asia and Africa. But what do the French and Swiss do? How is evangelization carried on in Spain and Sweden? True, the author does not describe the methods used by the nationals of any of these countries. But the reader has in his hands M. Kreitmann's method. It is less flamboyant than much American evangelization, but more serious and penetrating. Not only is his approach more suitable to Europeans, but I venture to believe that Americans would do well to adapt, adopt, and use it here.

Gordon H. Clark

THE TRANSLATOR

Mrs. Crumpacker, the translator, studied three years at Northwestern University and is a graduate of Butler University. In 1965 she received a Ph.D. in Foreign Languages and Literature at the Univesity of Chicago.

An Associate Professor at Valparaiso University where she has taught French since 1965, Mrs. Crumpacker is a frequent contributor to many periodicals.

Married to a civil engineer, she has two daughters and three grand-children. One daughter, Margaret, is a medical missionary in Hong Kong under the Evangelical Free Church.

BREAD, PEACE, and LIBERTY was published originally by Éditions "Le Phare," 5531 Flavion, Belgique in 1971.

THE AUTHOR

The author studied at the University of Paris where he received a Doctorate in Law and a diploma from the Free School of Political Science. Military service followed by the war of 1939-45 kept him in the army where he was made a major in the artillery. Taken prisoner in June, 1940, he remained behind barbed wire in Germany until 1945.

After the war he joined the Crédit Foncier de France, the main French land bank. Here he was given the responsibility of creating a special service of studies and methods for reorganizing this great loan-society for long-term credit and the perfecting of new operations. In 1951 he was named auditor for the Institute of Advanced Studies in National Defense, one of the youngest in the session. After this he left the land bank to manage various companies.

These professional responsibilities did not make him forget the importance of his spiritual life which had deepened in captivity through meditation on the Bible. Founder of the Centre de Formation Chrétienne, a Bible Institute for laymen, member of the board of directors of the French Bible Society, the Evangelical Alliance, and the Faculté Réformée de Théologie at Aix-en-Provence, he participated in several mass evangelism campaigns, especially with Billy Graham.

This competency in both political and spiritual matters makes him especially qualified to study in a new manner the present problem of bread, peace and liberty in the light of biblical revelation.

INTRODUCTION

The title of this work recalls the platform of the Popular Front which carried the day in the 1936 French legislative elections. The Communist, Socialist, and Radical-Socialist parties had joined forces to propose to the voters a platform which was summed up in these three words: "bread, peace, and liberty."

The politicians of these parties were clever. Several of them had received a brilliant education in the great French schools and universities. They pledged to the voters that, if they won the majority of the votes, they would form a government capable of giving to the French people in future years the bread, peace, and liberty they desired.

The French people who listened to these politicians and approved of their platform, as they indicated by their ballots in a free election, were not inexperienced politically. They had lived through several changes of regime since the 1789 Revolution. They were acquainted with democracy and should not have let themselves be swayed by political discourses.

Thus, four years after the 1936 elections these people and politicians, instead of obtaining the bread, peace, and liberty they were sincerely seeking, experienced just the reverse: severe food rationing, war, and bondage under the Hitlerian domination.

How could they have been so grossly deceived?

The purpose of this study is to discourage such errors in judgment, errors as pernicious for the conduct of nations as individuals. To accomplish this it looks beyond technological data, depending upon specialists for such information, while it seeks to set forth an intellectual position which is accurate, that is, free from deceitful illusion and founded on a sound appreciation of the historical evolution of our humanity. This work was carried out in the same spirit as *Le Maître de l'Histoire* (1966) by Jean André Blanc, the first in a series entitled "Le sens de l'Histoire."[1] One of the essential teachings of Blanc's work is that the reflections of the politicians, the elite, and of every individual who seeks to interpret events

---

[1] Éditions Le Phare, 5531 Flavion, Belgium.

fairly are bound to be false in every area if they fail to consider biblical revelation.

This study is made at a time when our world seems to be experiencing a new Renaissance and a new Reformation. All the foundations of our thinking are being called into question. Therefore, it is particularly opportune to reconsider our world's great problems in the light of the Bible. It will be an extraordinary discovery. Indeed, since the Council of Trent[2] and the Counter-Reformation,[3] the culture of the French-speaking countries has known almost nothing of the Bible. One need only read the curricula of the schools and universities along with the works of the principal masters of French thought to be stupefied by an almost complete silence in this regard. All give a large place to the ideas and philosophical systems of Greek, Latin, or modern origin. But on biblical thought one finds practically nothing except for a few brief citations isolated from their context. However, in the last few years more and more of the French elite have been discovering the Bible. Luxurious and popular editions now enable one to read this ancient work in good translations which can be compared with one another in order to find the most exact expressions. The number of its enthusiastic readers is increasing daily.

The consequences of this may be incalculable, for the Bible is no ordinary book. It is an inspired work, the Word of God written, which from the beginning to the end of its pages bears witness to an extraordinary man: Jesus Christ. By his love for humanity, his teaching, his sacrifice on the Cross, and by every witness to him in the biblical writings Christ appears truly as the one who bears the fullness of the living God, the Master of History. He is the Word of God made flesh who "dwelt among us, and we beheld his glory, glory as of the only begotten from the Father, full of grace and truth."[4] Through reading the Bible, one can therefore know Christ and find divine inspiration as well as the sovereign authority he

---

*[2]This ecumenical council (1543-63), which seems to have been prompted by the Protestant Reformation, solidified and unified Roman Catholic dogmas.   The reader will note that many of these footnotes are marked with an asterisk (*). In such cases, the notes have been added by the translator.

*[3]The Counter-Reformation of the sixteenth and seventeenth centuries corrected many abuses in the Roman Catholic Church but opposed the theological and biblical position of the Reformation. In particular, it insisted upon the dogmas of the Council of Trent which did not allow laymen to read the Bible by themselves.

*[4]John 1:14. All biblical references are from the New American Standard Version. Small case letters have been used for the pronouns referring to Christ and italics have been omitted.

needs not only for his faith, but also for his thinking and his entire life.

The present work constitutes only a modest stone to be brought to an edifice which needs to be built in the years to come. More than ever our world requires men and women of the Bible who will carry on and develop this work by adding other stones to this great building which will shed biblical light on all the domains of thought and action.

PART ONE

BREAD

"Dans la coupe arrondie à l'anse au col de cygne
Pose les fruits choisis sur des feuilles de vigne:
Les pêches qu'un velours fragile couvre encor,
Et les lourds raisins bleus mêlés aux raisins d'or.
Que le pain bien coupé remplisse les corbeilles . . .
Maintenant va chercher l'eau fraîche dans la cour
Et veille que surtout la cruche, à ton retour,
Garde longtemps, glacée et lentement fondue,
Une vapeur légère à ses flancs suspendue."[1]

(Aux flancs du Vase — Albert Samain.)

The term bread is to be taken here in its broad sense: it is the essential which every human being needs to survive, a simple but adequate nourishment as well as a modest but healthy lodging and decent clothing, suited to the climate.

Certainly this vital minimum may vary according to how temperate the regions are and how civilized the people. Lodging, clothing, and nourishment which satisfy primitive populations are not accepted by the poorest inhabitants of more advanced cultures where certain goods not necessary to life nevertheless come to be regarded as indispensable. A veritable perversion may even be produced in the appreciation of what is essential. For example, during the last war famished prisoners suffering from hunger were seen exchanging their meagre supplies of bread, insufficient as they were, for cigarettes.

---

*[1] In the curved cup with swan's-neck handle/Place the choicest of fruit on the vine leaves:/Peaches still covered with delicate velvet,/Heavy blue grapes mixed with grapes of gold./Let the baskets be filled with well-cut bread . . ./Now fetch fresh water from the courtyard/And make sure that the pitchers, upon your return./Retain for a long time, frozen and slowly melting/A slight vapor suspended on their sides.

The threshhold of the vital minimum therefore remains largely relative and subjective. Some will be happy in a thatched cottage leading a simple, temperate, and frugal life. Others, even though they already enjoy a real superfluity compared with the first, will bewail their lot while sincerely maintaining that they lack the necessities.

With this reservation, it is certain that obtaining daily bread has always been and remains the primary occupation of the great majority of men. The entire history of mankind demonstrates that very often bread happens to be cruelly lacking even in the midst of a prosperous society for individuals, underprivileged minorities, or the whole population of vast areas where malnutrition, dearth, and even famine are rampant. Therefore, it is important to set wise guidelines which would permit individuals as well as nations to avoid suffering, because some day they might lack bread. To understand the profound significance of the word bread today it is necessary to have experienced hunger oneself, to have felt the persistent gnawing of the stomach and the lack of vitality following restrictions which have been prolonged for weeks, months, and even years, and to have been grieved because of the limitations imposed upon one's own household.

Chapter 1

Man's Efforts to Assure Himself of the Vital Minimum

Standpoint of the individual: work, thrift, solidarity, insurance.

Even when a political revolution or slump causes a leveling which brings all the citizens to the same station, profound inequalities quickly reappear, creating once again a distinction between the rich and the poor.

Beginning at the same starting point, at the same social level, men are rapidly differentiated. Some waste all their income. Others, more far-sighted, save money. Their savings, wisely managed or favored by circumstances, can become considerable. People forget too easily today, after the loss of even modest fortunes following inflation, nationalization, the defection of foreign debtors, et cetera . . . . that by simply putting aside $100 a month for ten years at five percent interest, compounded monthly, they obtain a sum of $15,528.

Without our always being aware of it, the fable of "The Grasshopper and the Ant" is played out every day under our very eyes:

> The grasshopper gay
> Sang the summer away (Wright)
> And found himself starving
> On winter's first day. (G. H. Clark)[1]

But the notion of joint family responsibility, recognized and sanctioned by French civil code, obliges families who have such a "grasshopper" to come to his aid, thanks to the resources of the others. To be sure this is not always done very willingly.

Regular and persistent work, thrift, and foresight have always helped during hard times to guarantee the bread which is indispensable to life. Such practices have permitted many men and families throughout the ages to surmount the trials of life and to await the return of better days by making sufficient funds available, on the individual level or within the framework of joint family or group responsibility. These virtues have con-

---

*[1] The French poet, Jean de la Fontaine (1621-95), was best known for his *Fables* and *Contes.*

tributed to the formation of strong men and of great and solid families, whose presence is necessary for the life of nations.

But today such virtues seem to have been forgotten because man finds himself in the presence of another conception giving him the illusion of never lacking anything. Instead of remaining individual, saving tends to become collective. An obligatory saving is added to the voluntary one simultaneously or sometimes substituted for it.

Collective and enforced saving, realized by the different forms of social insurance, often presents serious inconveniences. Man always suffers from an externally imposed constraint while without a murmur he puts up with heavy burdens when he takes them on voluntarily. Moreover state systems of social security easily become clumsy, bureaucratic administrations which interfere in a vexatious, authoritarian, and inhuman manner, making relationships difficult and disappointing. And above all they do not generally cover the whole risk.

However, collective saving can assume yet another appearance. Its obligatory character does not necessarily imply the formation of a public or semi-public service. Thus liability insurance for motorists is generally taken care of by competitive private insurance companies, each vying with the other to give its clients the best service so as to receive the preference. In some countries, insurance for sickness, prolonged illness, old age, and unemployment likewise fall to private companies which try equally hard to please their clients.

It is important, under these conditions, to recognize the advantages of the various kinds of insurance which permit beneficiaries to obtain payments even when the accident happens suddenly before the individual savings has yet had time to accrue. The insurance complements the joint responsibility of the family or the social group, which already stretches the individual reserves. Moreover, it does so without suppressing these two forms of saving, a fact which is too easily forgotten. In the same way a joint liability of the entire national common ownership may be obtained with the form of reinsurance to which companies must subscribe in order to cover important risks.

The notion of saving seems to correspond to a profound instinct of nature, which is more perceptible in the case of insects than with men who are too often improvident. Even so, the notion of joint responsibility when applied at the family level, as well as at the national and international levels, arises from a conception of man which has not always existed and which is not recognized by all.

In antiquity a close solidarity existed on the family plane. The family was the basic cell of society and at the same time the fundamental religious community in which the gods of the hearth were worshiped. As Fustel de Coulanges pointed out so well, the entire social, legal, economic, and political organization of the city-state rested on this religious conception of the family cell.[2] The solidarity was very strong on the familial level of the clan or tribe. It was also the case on the level of the city-state, where the same gods were worshiped, but it did not go beyond its walls. With other men, worshipers of other gods, there existed only enforced relationships. The massacre of the wounded, of the prisoners, of the conquered, and the sad fate of slaves dispersed and sold like merchandise without taking into account their family ties, illustrate this in an unhappy way. Neither honesty nor truth went beyond the walls of the city-state, the safety of which was the supreme rule permitting and justifying every ruse and lie with respect to its enemies.

Such ideas impregnate more than we realize the mentality of our contemporaries and the laws of our modern States. The notion of familial solidarity, which was inherited from the ancients on the sustenance level, taken in the broad sense as we understand it here, figures in Articles 203 and following of the French Civil Code which legally sanctions joint responsibility for "bread" not only of parents for children, but also for all relatives including sons-in-law and daughters-in-law.

But it was necessary to wait more than a century after the drafting of the Civil Code for the appearance of the so-called social legislation: the extension of the concept of joint responsibility to national common ownership as a whole. An organic solidarity on the international level seems still less likely to be realized, but the idea is underway, supported by organizations like the Red Cross whose Christian and biblical inspiration in the person of its founder Henri Dunant cannot be denied.[3]

Biblical revelation leads indeed to a conception of man which is radically different from that of the city-states of antiquity. Affirming that all men are children of the same Father—rebellious ones to be sure, the Bible

---

[2]*La Cité antique,* Books II & III.

*[3]Henri Dunant (1828-1910) whose family fled to Geneva after the Revocation of the Edict of Nantes was an active evangelical Christian, he inspired, at the age of 29, meetings of young people who had been touched by the Awakening. In 1852, in Paris, he contributed to the founding of the YMCA.

extends the notion of joint responsibility to the entire world, giving the ant as an example of work and foresight:

> Go to the ant, O sluggard,
> Observe her ways and be wise,
> Which,having no chief,
> Officer or ruler,
> Prepares her food in the summer,
> And gathers her provision in the harvest.
> How long will you lie down, O sluggard?
> When will you arise from your sleep?
> "A little sleep, a little slumber,
> A little folding of the hands to rest"—
> And your poverty will come in like a vagabond,
> And your need like an armed man.
>
> (Prov. 6:6–11)

The Bible insists in many other passages similar to this one on the necessity of working to earn one's living. The laborious character of work is a consequence of man's revolt against his Creator:

> Cursed is the ground because of you;
> In toil you shall eat of it
> All the days of your life . . . .
> By the sweat of your face
> You shall eat bread.   (Gen. 3:17, 19)

It is therefore by submitting to this hard law of work that men succeed in procuring the bread they need for life. Any other conception would lead to serious disillusionment.

On the other hand, one must recognize that the Bible, with the exception of the passage relative to the ant mentioned above, insists little on the benefits and necessity of saving. Certainly the very familiar praise of the virtuous woman shows her purchasing a field and planting a vineyard.[4] It is what we today call productive investments which permit the expansion of family agricultural cultivation. The savings in reserve is also mentioned: the text specifies that the woman has foresight with respect to lean seasons and to lending a hand to the unfortunate and poor. This shows, on the one hand, that affluence according to the Bible never accompanies selfish enjoyment of material goods, but leads instead to mutual aid. Calvin justly named this attitude the ministry of the rich to the poor, em-

---

[4]Prov. 31:10-31.

phasizing the fact that one is always rich with respect to someone less favored than oneself.[5]

But numerous biblical texts recall with severity that one must guard against amassing riches in order to enjoy them selfishly. On the contrary the goods which God bestows upon the rich are to be utilized for Christian works, as well as to help the poor and unfortunate:

> Do not lay up for yourselves treasures upon earth, where moth and rust destroy, and where thieves break in and steal. But lay up for yourselves treasures in heaven, where neither moth nor rust destroys, and where thieves do not break in or steal; for where you treasure is, there will your heart be also.
>
> (Matt. 6:19–21)

> Come now, you rich, weep and howl! for your miseries which are coming upon you . . . . Behold, the pay of the laborers who mowed your fields, and which has been withheld by you, cries out against you; . . . You have lived luxuriously on the earth and led a life of wanton pleasure; . . . You have condemned and put to death the righteous man; he does not resist you.
>
> (James 5:1, 4–6)

These striking texts show the criminal gravity not only of acquiring riches dishonestly by depriving one's partners of their legitimate share, but also of failing to feel responsibility for those who lack even the necessities because one is too concerned with one's own comfort.

Other passages emphasize that love and service to one's neighbor are, in the mind of God, the means par excellence to accord him the worship that pleases him:

> Is this not the fast which I chose,
> To loosen the bonds of wickedness,
> To undo the bands of the yoke,
> And to let the oppressed go free,
> And break every yoke?
> Is it not to divide your bread with the hungry,
> And bring the homeless poor into the house;
> When you see the naked, to cover him;
> And not to hide yourself from your own flesh?
>
> (Isa. 58:6, 7)

---

[5]*Commentaries,* Acts 11:29.

Thus, biblical revelation lays stress, first of all, on the need for all to work to assure their own nourishment as well as that of others. It admits the merits of wholesome foresight, and especially of a productive economy. Moreover, it also insists strongly on the necessity of a true and real solidarity among all men, without familial and national limits, to assure to all the bread which is indispensable to life.

Therefore, the Christian cannot simply be satisfied with working whole-heartedly, intelligently, and conscientiously, with seeing that his co-laborers and workmen receive a just salary, and with coming personally with help to the needy. He must also, according to the will of God, work to bring about a true solidarity among all men. He will therefore give his support to the organization of social insurance and international mutual aid. But he will not be content with the impersonal and vexatious structures of a vast administration. Within his ability, he will make truly human and understanding every organization which contributes to the realization of a true solidarity among men.

The above considerations emphasize that each individual must carry personally a share of responsibility in the creating of goods required not only for his own subsistence, but also for that of others. He can respond to this responsibility by his willingness to work and by his conscientious labor, foresight, and social sense. But his efforts are useless on this last point if the government of each State in the world is not likewise clearly conscious of its responsibility in this area.

Standpoint of the government

Social justice, sufficient bread for all, and the prosperity of a nation depend in large measure on the competency of its government and the wisdom of its laws. One might say that each nation has the government it deserves. In primarily democratic countries the laws are the expression of the will of the majority of the citizens. There remains, none the less, an art of governing nations wisely, or, if one prefers, a political science which ought to form an integral part of the required training of statesmen; it is a science which comprises not only the knowledge of a certain number of political, juridical, or economic techniques and the comparative study of institutions and laws, but also a correct appreciation of man and the underlying motives for his action.

Such a science is not very widespread today. When one considers a prosperous nation, it is often as difficult now as it was in the past to distinguish between what is peculiar to its manner of governing itself and what might constitute general rules and instruction which could be transposed to another ethnic, geographical, and historical setting.

On the other hand, chiefs of State and government are generally party men subscribing to a whole set of political, economic, and social doctrines which are often rigid and purely theoretical and which either refuse to take notice of the fundamental teachings of a true political science or oppose them openly.

Happy are those nations which succeed in placing in power not cold doctrinaires, but persons having a true knowledge of man and economic realities. Happy especially are those men involved in politics who can combine the facts of objective experience and the knowledge of economic doctrines with the teachings of biblical revelation; the latter alone permits the acquisition of exceptional wisdom, intelligence, and discernment.[6] They will know how to lead their nations toward a harmonious prosperity and to protect them from hazards of every kind.

Different economic regimes

For several decades we have been seeing two very different political and economic regimes which claim by contrary principles to assure the happiness of the populations of very extensive areas of our globe.

On the one hand, the Eastern world of Marxist-Leninist inspiration condemns private property and initiative, advocating a vast State capitalism with a general leveling imposed by a totalitarian government.

On the other hand, the Western world, under the impetus of the United States, subscribes to doctrines of economic liberalism, trusting the individual; encouraging his liberty, profit, thrift, and initiative; emphasizing the favorable results of competition for the good of consumers; declaring that supply is automatically adapted to demand when suitable working conditions are assured in a free market; and limiting State intervention to a control and orientation of economic activity principally by means of currency, credit, and taxes. Levying taxes permits the realization of public works and other endeavors of national interest.

The profound imperatives of each of these systems are too often forgotten. Authoritarian planning implies a strong State which intervenes in the daily life of consumers, determining how they must dress, eat, or lodge themselves and which sends those who oppose it to concentration camps. Every attack against the system of authoritarian distribution becomes a

---

[6]Ps. 119:97-105.

crime against the nation. The fact that a peasant ate an egg from the farm where he works risks making him appear as an ordinary criminal before the tribunals of common law. Such a system is justified, however, in a period of great scarcity and national calamity when it is important to assure to each person the vital minimum. But when the danger is removed these extreme restraints become a stimulus to inactivity on the part of the workers, a curb on economic expansion, and a cause of immorality by the multiplication of opportunities for fraud and black marketing.

In periods of peace, the regime which appeals to private property and to the initiative and profit of each inhabitant of a country is the one which leads to the greatest prosperity. Figures comparing incomes per inhabitant of the different countries of the world are indisputable proof of this. But one must not forget that for an aggregate of producers and consumers to gain access to a free and competitive market it is often necessary to bring about deep-seated structural reforms which States with feudalistic regimes do not always dare to undertake. The agrarian reform which gives the ownership of the soil to those who cultivate it directly clashes with the interests of the great proprietors who manage huge farms. Liberty of commerce and industry breaks the routine of the trade guilds. Encouragement given to a productive economy carries a threat to the privileges of ancient families habituated to sumptuous expenditures. Finally, a regime of economic liberty presupposes a State which can voluntarily limit its interventions to a strict minimum and which causes liberty to reign on the political plane as great as it advocates on the economic one.

Thus the choice of an economic regime is an act which determines the prosperity of a nation. Biblical revelation gives no precise and imperative instruction on this subject—nor for the choice of a political regime. It seems that, except for the Israelites of Old Testament times, God wishes to leave men free in this domain or rather that he seeks more to define a spirit, or inspiration, than to prescribe rigid rules. According to this spirit, each regime will retain only a secondary and relative value valid in terms of the circumstances. The Christian is carefully put on guard against all idolatry including that of a political or economic regime. Moreover, in keeping with the same spirit he will always seek to humanize the regime in which he lives. In this way the Bible acknowledges the merits of property and individual responsibility. But it also underscores their limits and puts him on guard against abuses and possible deviations.[7] It insists on the dangers of

---

[7]See the interesting study of this question in *Le Maître,* part II, chap 1.

abundance as well as poverty, of the seduction of riches and the necessity of sharing one's bread with the hungry.[8]

Concern for assuring a material living to the masses seems too often not the first preoccupation of many governments which prefer to give priority to prestige, ideology, or other considerations. One must not be astonished under these conditions that many States of the Third World, and even of Europe, which have voluntarily made bad choices or have not known how to decide between two opposing regimes suffer from underdevelopment and even insufficient food as a result. Economic aid accorded such States is, in reality, a simple waste, like pouring water into a barrel with a hole in it before having taken the trouble to repair it.

Besides, the States which were able to give proof of wisdom in their choice of institutions do not need to cry for help. Their economic regimes give rise to confidence and their productive investments abound by themselves. The present examples of the Federal Republic of Germany or Switzerland and certain States of the Third World attest to this. Such fundamental truths seem to be easily forgotten today. One generally fails to recognize the first reponsibility of the nations which are stagnating in chronic underdevelopment, in Europe as well as on the other continents. The problem of the economic development of a nation arises in the last resort a great deal less from natural resources than from the state of mind of its population and the intellectual formation of its elite.[9]

The quality and competence of the rulers, as of responsible people at every echelon, will permit good institutions to function well, especially for: the regulation of economic activities, the determination of the optimum density of the population in a given territory, and the collective precautions to take in anticipation of perils which might threaten the life of the people.

The regulation of economic activities

In this regard human societies have passed through several stages. In still primitive economies the level of agricultural, industrial, and commercial activities remains subject primarily to natural hazards. Poor harvests, long periods of drought, ravages by insects, and military insecurity are sufficient to create severe penury. Prosperity returns with good harvests. States have succeeded in coming out of this primitive economy only by ac-

---

[8]Prov. 30:8-9; I Tim. 6:10; Ezek. 17:7.

[9]*Le Maître,* part III, end of chapter 1.

quiring enough power to ensure peace and security within their frontiers, by organizing the stocking of essential foodstuffs in periods of prosperity, and by maintaining a network of means of communication permitting them in short periods of respite to come to the aid of regions devastated by natural cataclysms.

Thus prosperity appears to be linked to the constitutions of powerful empires or, at least, to the realization of an agreement among nations having common economic aims. These conditions were realized, it seems, in antiquity at the time of the great Chinese, Babylonian, Egyptian, and other Empires, then in the West with the Roman Empire, and following the industrial revolution, in the nineteenth century.

Yet, in the course of the nineteenth century, with this revolution, the Western economy experienced again great economic crises periodically every seven to ten years. The last and most important was the crisis of 1929. Since then, governments have rightly abandoned their noninterference policy in order to control economic activity. This regulation is necessary and legitimate provided they take into account the mechanism which assures the functioning of free markets in which prices are fixed by the law of supply and demand. A sane intervention consists in acting on the supply or demand without interfering with the price machinery. On the contrary, state action would be disruptive if it took place by blocking or impeding the functioning of this mechanism without replacing it with a general systematic authoritarian planning. Here again one must know how to make judicious choices which will have a profound and durable impact on the prosperity of the people.

Ever since the end of the Second World War, the principal States of the Western world have tried to bolster economic activity, when it risks stagnating, by an expansion of public expenditures, credit, and money, or by slowing it down through opposite measures, if there appears a danger of ''overheating.'' But they did not prevent a permanent rise in prices, the sign of a chronic inflation which also discouraged private saving. As a consequence, beginning in 1974, when a veritable economic crisis was triggered by the brutal inflating of oil prices for reasons more political than economic, the regulatory system ceased to work. A galloping ''two-digit'' inflation became general along with significant unemployment. Rare are the countries which, like Switzerland, have succeeded in curbing both inflation and unemployment.

However, in the course of the last thirty years, the Western world has been successful not only in rapidly rebuilding all the war torn areas, but also in giving to its populations a standard of living never before attained.

Therefore, no one should question the effectiveness of the liberal economy, with its price machinery. But is a good regulation of the economy possible?

Apparently it was the money problem in particular which could not be resolved. From the internal standpoint a chronic inflation was deliberately accepted, leading people to live beyond their means and to neglect saving. Likewise, from an international perspective, it was not possible to have available a sound currency, a recognized means of exchange in which each State would have confidence and which ought also to be a good standard of values. In the nineteenth century it was thought that this standard of values had been found in precious metals, that is, gold and silver. But the unequal increase in their production threw the system off balance. It became necessary to call a halt to bimetalism by withdrawing silver from circulation. Only the gold standard was retained. But production of gold was insufficient to increase the amount of currency to keep up with the expanding economy; this risked leading to deflation, which is likewise productive of an economic crisis.

At the beginning of the twentieth century, the adoption of the "Gold Bullion Standard" and the "Gold Exchange Standard" permitted the reduction of the quantity of gold required for the functioning of the international money system. But, as a result of the great crisis of 1929, most States abandoned the gold standard between 1931 and 1936.

During the Second World War, the Bretton Woods monetary agreements of July 1944 reestablished a regime of fixed, exchange rates, subject to modifications and aid granted by an International Monetary Fund. Along with gold, the dollar and the pound sterling were recognized as reserve currency. The dollar was itself convertible into gold. Still, the rise in international trade brought to light the insufficiency of the international monetary liquidities. Just as, on the internal plane, the volume of means of payment can no longer be tightly bound to the gold balance of the issuing institute without instigating grave economic recessions; also, on the international plane it is likewise important to abandon the practice of using gold coins or bills to arrive at an international fiduciary currency the volume of which could be adapted to the general needs of the economy.

The creation of special minting rights, decided upon at the Stockholm Conference in March 1968 and applied since January 1970, was intended to bring a solution to this problem by permitting an increase in the resources of the International Monetary Fund independent of gold production. The question was then posed as to whether governments could be wise enough to use these resources properly.

Thus the international monetary system resulting from the Bretton Woods agreements assured a relative momentary stability for thirty-two years. Commerce was facilitated and greatly developed by these agreements. But in January 1976, the Jamaica Conference decided to leave the States free to fix for themselves the exchange-rate of their money or to let it fluctuate. The result, therefore, was a return to the erratic exchanges of the Thirties. This action was preceded by the 1971 decision to discontinue the convertibility of the dollar into gold, a decision which was caused by the persistent disequilibrium of the balance of payments of the United States since 1957. There had also been a devaluation of the dollar after the oil crisis in 1973.

Only the International Monetary Fund still exists. It can have a moderating influence on the variations of the exchange-rates, help the States which are temporarily in difficulty, and continue to issue special minting rights.

These monetary vicissitudes underscore the difficulty of regulating the economy in our rapidly evolving world. Besides, is not the alternation of abundance and dearth, of good and bad harvests, one of the laws of our life on earth to which we must adapt ourselves?

Generally speaking, if States, like some individuals, know how to manage their accounts well, regulate their expenditures in terms of their receipts, and provide the reserves necessary by encouraging thrift, they will have a wholesome economy and a strong currency which will inspire confidence and contribute to their prosperity. On the contrary, if they want to live beyond their means, if they do not possess the strength of character necessary to economize when circumstances require it, then their reserves will be used up and they will finish by falling into dire poverty. It is in the spirits and hearts of men, much more than in the methods of economic and monetary systems, that the real cause of inflation is to be found, as well as the difficulty of surmounting the crises with which we shall always be faced from one moment to the next.

The development of the countries of the Third World also rests upon the same principles. To a certain extent these countries are dependent upon international contingency. But, more than anything, it is their behavior and their judicious choices which are decisive. It is up to them to manage their budgets wisely without hurling themselves into sumptuous expenditures beyond their means; to see to making their currency worthy of trust internally as well as internationally by avoiding both monetary inflation and deflation; to choose a liberal economic regime favorable to initiative which promotes progress; and, especially, to work zealously and intelligently without spending all of their income day by day. Furthermore, these States must bring about the internal reforms needed to replace the feudal or tribal institutions with structures which encourage private initiative and the proper functioning of free markets. They must also guide productive activities toward a harmonious expansion of all their resources. Many recall the difficulties these countries suffered when on the great markets there was a fluctuation in the price of the raw materials of which they were the principal suppliers. Although these fluctuations are indispensable for adapting supply to demand, the producing countries suffer from them only insofar as they have committed the error of giving themselves over to monoculture. One of the first measures to take in such a case would be to increase their capacity for stocking and diversifying their agricultural products, to give priority to the internal market and to develop local convertible industries. This reconversion of the economy can be directed, within the framework of flexible state planning, principally through credit, customs duties, and taxes.

The optimum density of the population

The size of the population needed to develop a given region is also an important element of prosperity. For a long time this problem has been posed in simple terms. The economy lacked hands either for working the land or for industry and commerce. Vast territories remained uncultivated. Great natural riches were not being exploited. Therefore, the governments, which were concerned about the well-being and prosperity of their States sought to increase the population by attracting foreigners who could later become good citizens. This wise policy, which was practiced in the nineteenth century by the United States, is one of the reasons for its present prosperity. It is still in force in countries like Canada and Australia. Even in Europe since the last world war numerous foreigners have gone to Germany, Belgium, France, and Switzerland. This movement was slowed down or even reversed following the increase in unemployment due to the crisis set in motion by the rise in oil prices. But inversely certain States, especially in the Far East, suffer from a population which is too dense for their present possibilities of economic expansion. Japan appears to have succeeded in a remarkable manner in controlling overpopulation while assuring the exploitation of all its soil resources, enabling it to become one of the major economic powers in the world. Its example ought to inspire the other Asiatic States which suffer from overpopulation. The remedy consists of intense agricultural and industrial modernization along with a strict policy of birth control.

Indeed with present technical means it is possible to augment agricultural yields significantly; to increase the quantity of arable lands, primarily by irrigation;[10] and to intensify maritime deep-sea fishing considerably. As a result, a much larger population can be supported on a given soil than before, even without taking into account all the resources of industrial development which permit buying supplies abroad in exchange for manufactured products and services. In this way some countries have succeeded in expanding their agricultural production by 50 percent in the last 50 years. Still more spectacular results could be achieved if the people understood better how to ascertain their nutritional needs and to organize their agricultural production accordingly. The cultivation of a substance like chlorelle ought to be widespread:

> Chlorelle, a tiny sweet-water algae, transforms almost the total amount of the solar energy it receives into vegetable matter. In 12 hours it quadruples its weight. Its yield is 19 1/2 tons per acre per year, roughly ten times more than that of wheat. An area five miles square would produce enough to furnish 80 million people with an adequate ration of protein. Chlorelle contains six times more protein than rice, 30 times more vitamin A than calves liver and four times more vitamin C than the spinach which it resembles in taste.[11]

Thus it seems perfectly possible to struggle effectively against every threat of famine or simple malnutrition in the different parts of the world on the condition that the States which run such risks know how to make correct choices when it comes to economic regime, agricultural policy, and demographic control.

A strict birth control policy is imposed at present in several parts of the globe. It is indeed important not to let populations multiply in a thoughtless manner. Each country has an optimum population density which it must endeavor to attain but not exceed under penalty of leading entire populations into congested living conditions which make one think of concentration camps. Man needs enough space with greenery and silence in order to lead a free and responsible life. Population control is a new preoccupation for humanity, for governments as well as for each individual and

---

[10]Some regions in the Far East and North Africa, at present arid and barren, were formerly covered with rich vegetation, thanks to a perfected network of irrigation canals. Perhaps this example will encourage the many peoples who complain of the unprofitableness of their soil to do something about it.

[11]"L'Alchimie alimentaire," *Courrier de l'UNESCO,* July-August, 1969, p. 49.

home. In fact, up to the last century mankind was periodically ravaged by wars, famines, and epidemics. But in the twentieth century, even if wars and famines continue, the great epidemics which used to cause immense devastation are fast disappearing, thanks to the progress of medicine and hygiene. Each man's life expectancy is likely to double. This fact, together with the diminution of infant mortality, is one of the principal reasons for the present demographic explosion. And so humanity no longer finds itself confronted by a chronic shortage of populations but, on the contrary, the risk of overpopulation. At the same time the encouragement of large populations has ceased to be a military imperative. Power is no longer measured by the number of soldiers. With modern armaments a few resolute combatants stop a column of tanks. A curtain of atomic bombs would dislocate the vastest armies.

The control of demographic expansion, therefore, becomes mandatory with some overpopulated States. Modern techniques permit achieving this goal in an efficient manner. The people of these States can be encouraged to accept a regulation of births in harmony with the needs of the country. A rise in the standard of living which parallels instruction in birth control will also contribute effectively to making the need for this kind of regulation understood. It is sufficient to consider the example of France in the nineteenth century.

Men now have the power to procure for themselves proper nourishment and all that is essential for daily life. They are capable of forging for themselves the living conditions they desire. But will they be able to use this power wisely?

Anticipating dangers

To govern is to foresee. Unfortuntely this maxim of political wisdom is not always present to the minds of the rulers who often confine themselves to forecasting on a short-term basis and refuse to open their eyes to the long-range dangers their people may face.

To assure each person daily bread under all circumstances, it is not enough to realize a satisfactory volume of economic activity sufficient to avoid crises and to tend toward full employment, nor to see that the population density does not exceed the danger quota. It is still essential to think of catastrophes which may occur in an unusual manner, although with a certain regularity, every five, 10, 20, or 50 years. These are the great international political crises which sometimes end in regional or world wars. These crises are manifested immediately by a brutal breakdown of international trade. For Western nations the resulting regime of comparative national self-sufficiency would require immediate food and energy restrictions. For poorly industrialized nations these periods of crisis would entail grave difficulties in supplying spare parts for all machines and in purchasing industrial products. To reduce the incidence of such crises, foresighted governments will think of stocking the commodities most necessary to their nations. These stocks should be adequate to allow the nation to be self-sufficient for several years, taking into account the restrictions to be imposed and the possible increase in national production. In Switzerland during the last war, the Wahlen plan permitted a considerable increase in national agricultural production. Even the public parks were transformed into vegetable gardens. This tiny country gives another noteworthy example of foresight by the importance of the stockpiles of food products and combustible liquids and solids which were instituted by public means. Private persons were also requested to prepare permanent individual reserves of provisions.

Scientific and technological progress has considerably facilitated the realization of food stockpiles: canned produce and beverages, powdered soups, dehydrated, freeze-dried, and precooked food. Moreover, the prime cost of basic food products is normally very low, when one considers the threats of overproduction in Western countries. The building of stockpiles is, therefore, all the easier and more opportune in calm periods, since these conditions will be quickly reversed in a period of crisis.

Foreseeing the danger of war involves still other imperatives. Stockpiles will have to be scattered and protected against threats of destruction and denaturation by atomic, bacteriological, or chemical weapons. The establishment of subterranean depots helps to guard against these dangers.

In the same way the protection of the population in wartime poses complex problems because of the destructive power of modern arms. If the necessary precautions are not taken, large crowds are likely to find themselves suddenly without shelter, spare clothing, food, or medical care, and threatened with epidemics, should they escape total annihilation. Then they will truly lack their daily bread. In order to guard against such disasters, a long-range plan is mandatory.

The modern techniques which have allowed the fabrication of massive destructive arms likewise facilitate taking protective measures. The preventive dispersion of a large portion of city dwellers to the country, particularly women and children, is greatly simplified by the increasing number of country homes which the inhabitants of large cities are acquiring. This tendency is further facilitated by the reduction of the seven-day work week brought about by automation.

On the strictly protective level factories and various establishments are now being constructed, without any thought of defense, having total air conditioning which isolates them completely from the exterior atmosphere. Under these conditions one step more is needed to provide for their subterranean or even submarine installation. These steps would guarantee total protection. Such buried structures could prove income-producing even in peacetime since they liberate an area of high-priced land to the open air.[12] The carrying out of these kinds of plans should be systematically encouraged for key industries and essential establishments: hospitals, warehouses for provisions, et cetera. Communication by subway between these establishments would lead to the perfecting of truly subterranean and invulnerable cities. Because delays in warning are practically nonexistent, it would be possible to disperse the population of a country to its secondary residences and its buried cities to withstand any attack. This is not a question of an imaginary, futuristic vision but an objective which is perfectly realizable both technically and economically.

Carrying out an entire complex of measures for the protection of the population involves the construction of numerous individual and collective shelters as well. The price of such structures might seem prohibitive at first sight. But it is nothing of the sort if these projects are integrated with the rest of the peacetime works. Without great additional expense, basements of new apartment buildings, underground garages, subways, and various tunnels can easily be designed to be converted, when the time comes, into atomic-bomb shelters.

Instead of closing one's eyes to the possibility or asserting without serious argument that there will be no more war, the rulers of many countries would do better to face the facts.[13] They bear the responsibility for innumerable victims and immense suffering which could be avoided if a patient, systematic, and resolute policy were tenaciously pursued for facing the perils of war. Moreover such a policy constitutes a psychological deterrent which must not be underestimated. Here again, in the presence of atomic risks, man has available great possibilities for providing himself with an effective, if not absolute, protection. It is upon himself, his lucidity, his foresight, and his effort that his future seems to depend.

In the presence of the vital problem of daily bread, contemporary man

---

[12]See the interesting article by Lucien Barnier in *L'opinion économique et financière,* April 11, 1968. The address is La Vie Française-L'Opinion, 2 rue du Pont-Neuf, 75001 Paris.

[13]This subject will be developed more fully in Part II on Peace.

no longer depends upon the whims of nature. He can harness natural forces and make them serve him. He can also foresee and resolve problems raised by his life in society. Such power is the result of the long history, of humanity's slow ascent which has been accelerating for two centuries, thanks to technological and scientific advances. This progress would be full of promise if man were good and wise and if one could trust him to utilize the immense power he now possesses to assure the happiness of mankind by a harmonious development of natural resources. This hope has succeeded in intoxicating many of our contemporaries. It dominated the heart and mind of the Western world at the end of the nineteenth century and apparently still exists with those who ascribe to Marxist ideology.

But many men, women, and young people of today no longer have such confidence. They have been too bruised and disappointed by the last two world wars, which have bloodied for long years the so-called civilized nations. They have been scandalized by the abominable concentration-camp type of rule set up by nazism, fascism, and Marxist socialism. They see today, in all parts of the world, how rarely one finds true international solidarity, well directed States, honest administration, and people who are hard-working and peaceable. And they are now coming to the point of wondering whether man will misuse the great power available to him by making himself the victim of his own scourges, scourges which might prove much more frightful than the simple freaks of nature whose plaything he sometimes felt he was.

Chapter 2

Generally Forgotten Food:
The Bread of Life

The previous chapter ended with the distressing question of whether man would really be wise enough to utilize effectively the available means to assure bread for all. The important facts of our recent history, like those of everyday life, might cause one to doubt it.

It is here that a generally forgotten food should be mentioned. "Man shall not live on bread alone, but on every word that proceeds out of the mouth of God."[1]

And Jesus, the Christ, added:

> I am the bread of life; he who comes to me shall not hunger, and he who believes in me shall never thirst.[2]

The future of the world appears so somber because the great majority of our contemporaries in the West, as well as those in the East, fail to remember the necessity for the bread of life. They think of their material needs; they develop their strength; they count on themselves; and they believe that God is only an outmoded superstition, dead, good for a few old men set in out-of-date traditions and victims of a nonscientific education, or even for some young people who are behind the times, lost and incapable of taking their place in modern society. But one dimension is missing in their universe. Consequently, in spite of all their knowledge, studies, diplomas, and intellectual aptitudes, they do not possess the true intellectual capacity to understand fully the world's dramatic changes, the secret and profound malady of sin which gnaws at our humanity, and the emptiness of their own hearts. To acquire this intelligence they would have to have a different nourishment, a food which is within reach of every man, but which is ignored or scorned: the bread of life.

---

[1] Matt. 4:4.
[2] John 6:35.

What is this Bread?

It is not possible to go on here to study the Bible's exceptional character compared with all the other books written by men, the source of its spiritual authority, and its basic teachings.[3] Christ's two statements quoted in the preceding paragraph state clearly enough what constitutes the bread of life which every man needs more than vitamins or proteins. Such spiritual food is different from material goods which by themselves do not really satisfy man's deepest hunger. Twenty centuries ago Christ was already warning against a "society of consumers" who would lack the vision to look beyond their material needs to a great ideal.

Not every ideal can fulfill the hope of the human heart. The significance of the "bread of life" in the verse quoted above is twofold: it refers to "every word of God" meaning all the teachings of the Bible and to the Word made flesh or the person of Christ. In spite of appearances to the contrary, there is no divergence or opposition between these two definitions. The Bible remains a human book conferring no spiritual life on the one who reads it superficially without discerning that from beginning to end it gives witness to the very person of Jesus Christ, Savior and Lord of all, and without seeking the help of the Holy Spirit whom Christ sends to his disciples to help them understand its profound meaning.[4]

Conversely, Christ told his disciples to study the Scriptures to understand everything that pertained to him.[5] And so one cannot validly approach the Bible without the revelation of Christ; neither can one know Christ without the Bible. The close union of both in the heart of the repentant and pardoned believer leads to the ineffable reality of the very presence of God in the heart of the regenerate man. This presence is central to saving faith.[6]

Practically speaking, how can this be accomplished? One must simply follow the rules given in the Bible and, more particularly, in the third chapter of John's Gospel. Many people have not understood this essential teaching nor have they wanted to listen to it. Jesus explains to Nicodemus, one of the Jewish leaders of the period, that it is necessary to be born again. It is a question of spiritual birth. For this to be possible, it first was necessary for Christ to be crucified in order to expiate the sin of mankind and for him to be raised again to manifest the victory of God

---

[3]On this subject see *Le Maître,* pp. 9-48 and other specialized works.

[4]Luke 24:44-45; John 20:22.

[5]Luke 4:16-21; 16:31; 24:27; et cetera.

[6]John 14:23.

and to give eternal life. Thus everything for the salvation of men is prepared by God. Men can refuse or accept this salvation freely, in circumstances which vary for each individual. The one who decides to accept it must recognize that he is a sinner, in rebellion against God and living a meaningless life which leads to death; and he must repent of this. He is then able to regard by faith the crucified and risen Jesus Christ. This regard is one of love and gratitude in response to the immense love which God first manifested for him by allowing his only Son to die on the cross in his place. When love arises in the heart of a future husband or wife everything generally begins with a simple glance. A new life and a marvelous love story begin in the same way with God who keeps his promises. Every sin is then pardoned and cleansed by Jesus Christ's sacrifice, a sacrifice which was accomplished once for all at Golgotha. Under the action of the Holy Spirit a spiritual regeneration is produced. It is the beginning of a great adventure: the life of a child of God who is happy to have found his Father again and to work beside him from now on throughout eternity always able to count on God's help as well as the power and inspiration of the Holy Spirit. A new man is born. His heart and his spirit are going to be transformed through day-by-day contact with Jesus Christ. By prayer and the reading of the Bible, he receives the bread of life in abundance.

Today, after long centuries of preparation, spiritual nourishment is within the reach of all. Ever since the drama of man's revolt against God and the Fall, it has been foretold that man might one day be able to get out of the unfortunate situation in which he had been placed.[7] Then the children of Israel, in the course of their desert wanderings in Sinai under the leadership of Moses nearly 1500 years before Jesus Christ, began to understand that by placing themselves under the care of God alone they obtained, however it might happen, the material food they required. Even in the midst of the driest desert they could each morning gather around the camp the manna which served them as bread: "Every man gathered as much as he should eat."[8]

The same teaching was repeated by Christ to all those who had come to listen to him when, on two occasions, he multiplied for them a few loaves of bread and some fishes, thereby nourishing a great crowd with minimal resources. He was able to declare with convincing force:

> Do not be anxious then, saying, "What shall we eat?" or "What shall we drink?" or "With what shall we clothe ourselves?"

----

[7]Gen. 3:1-19, especially v.15.
[8]Ex. 16:14-18.

> For all these things the Gentiles eagerly seek; for your heavenly
> Father knows that you need all these things. But seek first his
> kingdom and his righteousnes; and all these things shall be
> added to you.[9]

Thus whoever believes in Jesus Christ and seeks in him true spiritual food, is delivered from undue anxiety concerning his daily bread. He knows that he has in heaven an all-powerful Father and that he can confidently call upon him every day for his daily needs. Through prayer and trust even his work is liberated from the curse of sin. To be sure, it remains necessary and toilsome. The law of God clearly emphasizes the necessity for labor as well as Sabbath rest. But the work is accomplished in an altogether different spirit, not by constraint but voluntarily, not in a selfish manner, but out of love for God and one's neighbor. Many biblical tales, all impregnated with Oriental poetry, show that work performed in obedience to God is the object of his blessing. While that notion is very foreign to our materialistic society, it is worth the trouble to reread these narratives with care to grasp their spiritual meaning which is still valid today.

At the end of the reign of David, Israel's greatest king and a man after God's own heart, and again, at the beginning of the reign of Solomon, the children of Israel enjoyed a prosperity which was truly astonishing for such a small nation.

> Judah and Israel were as numerous as the sand that is on the
> seashore in abundance; they were eating and drinking and re-
> joicing. Now Solomon ruled over the kingdoms from the River to
> the land of the Philistines and to the border of Egypt; . . . and
> he had peace on all sides round about him.[10]

Thus God's promises and blessings were accomplished when the Israelites, after a painful, forty-year sojourn in the desert, entered the land of Palestine, the land which had been given to them as an everlasting inheritance:

> And all these blessings shall come upon you and overtake you
> if you will obey the Lord your God. Blessed shall you be in the
> city, and blessed shall you be in the country. . . . And the Lord
> will make you abound in prosperity, in the offspring of your body
> and in the offspring of your beast and in the produce of your
> ground, in the land which the Lord swore to your fathers to give

---

[9]Matt. 6:31-33.
[10]I Kings 4:20-21, 24.

you. . . . The Lord will open for you his good storehouse, the heavens, to give rain to your land in its season and to bless all the work of your hand. . . .[11]

King Solomon was also able to sing of the reality of God's blessings:

Unless the Lord builds the house,
They labor in vain who build it;
Unless the Lord guards the city,
The watchman keeps awake in vain.
It is vain for you to rise up early,
To retire late,
To eat the bread of painful labors;
For he gives to his beloved even in his sleep.[12]

The fulfillment of such great promises is stamped on the soil and history of Palestine. Archeologists and historians find evidence everywhere of the past prosperity of this country. Excavations reveal traces of former wells and irrigation canals which permitted the fertilization of a soil which was covered with vines, olive trees, majestic cedar forests, and green, flowering prairies where numerous flocks grazed. In the words of the Bible, milk and honey flowed in abundance.

The contrast with the arid areas and deserts of today is striking. One is still more astonished to read in the Bible the textual prophecy of the radical change in the character of the land of the Israelites and of their dispersion among the nations. This occurred when God withdrew his blessing from his people who, instead of obeying him, gave themselves over to idolatry, lewdness, injustice, lying, and selfish pleasures.

For the mountains I will take up a weeping and wailing,
And for the pastures of the wilderness a dirge,
Because they are laid waste, so that no one passes through,
And the lowing of the cattle is not heard;
Both the birds of the sky and the beasts have fled; they are gone.
. . . Why is the land ruined, laid waste like a desert, so that
no one passes through? And the Lord said, ''Because they have
forsaken my law which I set before them, and have not obeyed
my voice but have walked after the stubbornness of their heart.''[13]

This extraordinary history of the chosen people is given as a lesson and warning for all the nations of the earth.[14] Now that the bread of life, Jesus

---

[11]Deut. 28:2-12.
[12]Ps. 127:1-2.
[13]Jer. 9:10-14.
[14]I Cor. 10:6-11.

Christ, is no longer reserved for the Israelites, all the earth's inhabitants are invited to be nourished with it.[15] In this spiritual food they will find healing for their sicknesses and for the sin of which they are often unconscious along with a new strength, a spirit and intelligence which was utterly foreign to them, peace of mind, and a capacity, unknown until then, for loving God as a tender Father and their neighbors, even their enemies, as brothers.

The fact that on earth, on every continent and among all races, there are men and women who are nourished with such a bread can have incalculable consequences, although the public press and the official radio and television scarcely seem to notice them.

What happens to men and nations who are nourished with the bread of life?

From the great examples of the past and the teachings of Christ it becomes clear that men and women who are nourished with the bread of life have within themselves a veritable regenerative power which transforms their internal being. This change can be instantaneous, but it can also be accomplished slowly step by step. In any case, the old man disappears in order to leave room for a man radically new, not only pardoned but also cleansed from sin and liberated from its chains, with a heart and mind in the image of Jesus Christ.[16]

Today this new humanity is not one well defined people, geographically localized with its ethnic type and history. It cannot even be identified with any of the various Christian churches or even with those who call themselves Christians, whatever may be the eccesiastical confession to which they belong. Indeed, the churches often have all too human traditions, ways of life, and rites. The bread of life can fail to be recognized because of false doctrines, spiritual indifference, and worldly preoccupations.[17] As a matter of fact, the true people of God are not numerous. They are dispersed not only among the various churches but also among all the nations of the earth. Certain churches and nations are thick with them; others have far fewer. In some regions these true children of God are numerous, respected and loved. The Bible, in which they find their spir-

---

[15]Mark 16:15.

[16]I John 1:9; Gal. 5:1.

[17]For more details see *Le Maître*, 2nd ed. part II. See also E. Jordan and J. Kreitmann, *Abrégé de l'Histoire de l'Eglise chrétienne.* The address is Editions Le Phare, 5531 Flavion, Belgium.

itual bread, is widely distributed and placed within the reach of all. Elsewhere they are persecuted, imprisoned, tortured, and massacred. Naturally the Bible is forbidden, confiscated, and burned.

Such a dispersion within human society is determined by God: "You are the salt of the earth; . . . the light of the world," said Christ to his disciples.[18] And the apostle stated explicitly: "Do all things . . . that you may prove yourselves to be blameless and innocent, children of God above reproach in the midst of a crooked and perverse generation, among whom you appear as lights in the world, holding fast the word of life."[19]

Salt is consumed in minute quantities compared with the total consumption of food. But its presence is sufficient to change the savor of the food. It is the same with true Christians for the society in which they live. In order to understand the essential and irreplaceable contribution which true, spirit-fed Christians make to a nation or a city, we must be explicit when we compare them with unbelievers and the many pseudo-Christians with whom we come in contact every day. The latter, as a matter of fact, are not Christians at all in the biblical sense; that is, they do not have Christ living in their hearts and do not faithfully keep his word.[20]

The characteristics of true Christians may be summed up by the following four essential traits.

—Work

Most men work because they must, driven by the necessity which obliges them to earn their living. Some come to be attached to this work which occupies the major part of their existence and thoughts. But the great majority prefer to be relieved of the responsibility most occupations entail as soon as the opportunity presents itself. Once free, they think nothing of letting their load weigh doubly on the shoulders of others who are reduced to true drudgery. Work can also be the means of gratifying one's ambitions and passions. It allows access to posts where one is surrounded by privileges and honors. This glory easily intoxicates, and to attain it some men are ready to go to great effort and sometimes to employ shameful means. In their battle to achieve power they often conceal a callous ruthlessness with a superficial amiability and politeness.

The true Christian, on the contrary, works in an unselfish manner. He

---

[18]Matt. 5:13-14.

[19]Phil. 2:14-16.

[20]For a discussion of the spiritual qualities of these Christians, see *Le Maître*, part II, chapter 3.

seeks an activity in which he can do his share and help his neighbor to the best of his ability. Work is indeed a real ministry for him: his profession is the privileged place where his love for God and others is given its foremost expression. He devotes his heart and mind to it, asking God's blessing upon it. We saw above how full of significance and promise the word blessing is. Thus all those who have business with one of these men know that they can count on him and trust him. They notice quickly that he does not do his work in a perfunctory manner with an eye on the clock but that he accomplishes it with heart and intelligence. Under these conditions men and women of the Bible find themselves rapidly promoted to posts of trust and responsibility. Because these qualities can rarely be found today, they often arouse envy, jealousy, and slander. Was it not foretold that Christians would always be persecuted?[21] But it is fitting to emphasize that it is not their personal qualities and capabilities, even when they are developed in obedience to God's commandments, which make the achievements of these men so valuable. It is the fact that through prayer and meditation on the Word they lean daily upon the living God, Creator of heaven and earth.

> And it is he who changes the times and the epochs;
> He removes kings and establishes kings;
> He gives wisdom to wise men,
> And knowledge to men of understanding.
> It is he who reveals the profound and hidden things;
> He knows what is in the darkness,
> And the light dwells with him.[22]

Happy are the nations, happy are all undertakings which recognize the value of such men and are assured of their cooperation.[23]

—Liberty

Knowing that his daily bread is given to him by his heavenly Father, the Christian is relieved of worry so far as his material life is concerned.[24] He works conscientiously, earnestly, and lovingly, as it has just been pointed out, but with a spirit of voluntary involvement which removes internal anxiety and permits him to adopt a social behavior free from all servility.

---

[21] II Tim. 3:12. See also the story of Joseph (Gen. 39).

[22] Dan. 2:21-22.

[23] For a concrete illustration of this kind of behavior in life and work read the novel *On ne m'a pas jeté la pierre* by A. Dufour (Editions Le Phare).

[24] Matt. 6:11 25-34.

Thus he will not be ruthlessly engaged in the struggle for power or maximum profit for he scorns the honors and riches of this world, having all his glory in Jesus Christ. He is no longer enslaved to money or earthly passions. He loves to live simply and soberly, for he finds in Jesus Christ the fullness of inner joy. But he will try to come to the aid of his most handicapped comrades at work and to his suffering and unfortunate neighbors.

He will know how to say no, without vehemence or anger but peaceably and with firmness, to his working companions as well as to his superiors or associates when they want him to participate in an act which is contrary to justice or condemned by his conscience. Such an attitude is both formidable in opposition to those for whom the end justifies the means and beneficial for all the others who, in the mêlée of self-interest and confused spiritual values, will finally locate a solid and fixed point to which they can refer.

Because of his stand the Christian will have to face a veiled and permanent hostility on the part of certain people. He will risk suffering from intrigues and slander of all kinds. But he will not fear losing his position, if need be, for he knows that he can count on the unfailing support of his heavenly Father who is "greater than all."[25] He was warned in advance that he would have tribulation in the world, but he has a powerful protector permitting him to walk like a conqueror whatever the circumstances.[26] In like manner the Apostle Paul could let himself be thrown into prison and be uncertain what the next day might hold without losing his peace and inner freedom.[27]

—Truth

The Christian who follows biblical teaching diligently attaches a great importance to truth and to the honesty which is its corollary. In fact, for him, truth is one of the attributes of divinity: "I am the way, and the truth, and the life," Jesus Christ declared.[28] Contrariwise, lying is Satanic: "But let your statement be, 'Yes, yes!' or 'No, no'; and anything beyond these is evil."[29] Thus, not only the outright lie is categorically condemned, but also all of its indirect forms, notably the mental restriction which was so cleverly codified by the Jesuits and which appears very spontaneously in human conduct.

---

[25]John 10:29.
[26]John 16:33.
[27]Acts 16:23-25.
[28]John 14:6.
[29]Matt. 5:37.

Under these conditions the battle for truth is both very simple and very difficult. It is simple because the choice between God and Satan must be made without equivocation. One is veracious or one is not. There are no half-truths, no ironical statements intended to convey the contrary; in fact, these are euphemisms which disguise the lie. Of course, one must know how to tell the truth at the right time in love with the necessary consideration for feelings. Since one must never lie, it may be opportune to remain silent at times.

The fight for truth is very arduous because our society rests more than people realize on a whole tissue of lies which one really discovers only on the day one has resolved not to lie any more. In social relationships how many lies there are under the veil of politeness! In work relationships great strength of character is needed to spurn false declarations of all sorts. Thus at times it seems as if one is going down a blind alley. How difficult it is to disentangle oneself from a false situation which has at its foundation one first untrue statement, which led to many others as a consequence! This is where one clearly discerns the work of Satan who knows so well how to entice victims in order to forge their chains more securely. As a matter of fact the fight for truth is a fight against Satan in person who will know how to display all of his charms, ruses, and ability to intimidate in order to break down those who dare to oppose him. That is why it behoves a person not to count only on his own strength but to implore without ceasing the help of the Lord who will then intervene to fortify and guide his weak disciple. A solution will appear even in the most hopeless situations. The light will dawn. And those who are resolved to walk unfalteringly in truth and honesty will avoid much pain and anguish. Much more, they will contribute, at times without realizing it, to transforming and purifying the environment in which they are called to live. They will also encourage just and wholesome enterprises and will discourage dishonorable work.

—Fraternity

The most extraordinary consequence of faith in Jesus Christ, when it penetrates a heart, is to destroy selfishness. In the natural state, man is intensely self-centered. He thinks the world revolves around him. He organizes his entire life for his own advantage and interest. Even his actions which seem to be unselfish are not so in reality. He seeks to acquire a good reputation. He wants to have a good opinion of himself. The natural man may even seek certain advantages in the so-called selfless services he renders because he anticipates gratitude and a reciprocal obligation.

A genuine miracle is necessary to transform this selfish heart into a loving and brotherly heart. Only the revelation of the unfathomable love of God, manifested in Jesus Christ dying on the Cross, can give a clear vision of the blackness of our sin and the abyss of our wickedness. The love of God penetrates the heart with pardon, overwhelms it, and brings it new feelings. Man reconciled to God learns to love in his turn. He will love his family, friends, and comrades at work in an entirely new manner. Step by step he learns to love men of all races and social conditions and to feel himself a brother to them. He will even love his enemies.[30]

Practically speaking, such a state of mind can have great repercussions on political, economic, and social life. It is among Christians that one finds the principal pioneers of all the great charitable and fraternal undertakings. It was a Christian, the industrialist Daniel Legrand, a friend of Pastor Oberlin,[31] also well known for his social work in France, who promoted social legislation—particularly the prohibition of child labor and the establishment of Sabbath rest. Daniel Legrand likewise pioneered that international work legislation which led to the creation of the International Labor Office (ILO) in Geneva. In the ILO headquarters a medallion in his memory was unveiled in 1927.

As we have seen, it was also a Christian, deeply pious and active in his evangelical church, Henri Dunant, who founded the International Red Cross.

Christians are called to act everywhere in the world to feed the famished and to clothe and lodge those who lack the essentials.[32] They must also speak up at their place of work and in their city or village, encouraging just wages for each worker and aid where needed for the retired, the old, the incurable, and all the helpless. They will have to struggle against social plagues and moral corruption.

Much more, knowing that material bread and clothing are not enough, Christians have it on their hearts to present to all men on earth the bread of life and the white robes of salvation. They have this concern for all men: in their family, their profession, their city, and their fatherland, but also to the ends of the world.

---

[30]On this subject read Matt. 5:44-47; Rom. 12:17-21.

*[31]Jean Frédéric Oberlin (1740-1826), an Alsatian clergyman and philanthropist, was celebrated for his services to the population of Ban de la Roche, among whom he labored for 60 years. He made roads, improved the system of agriculture, and promoted education. At the time of the French Revolution Ban de la Roche was saved through the reputation of the people and their pastor. Oberlin College, Ohio, was named for him.

[32]Isa. 58:7.

Work, liberty, truth, fraternity—these are the four essential characteristics of true Christians. But, someone will say, these virtues are not encountered among Christians only. Do not atheists and some who hold to
other religions lead exemplary lives as well and practice these virtues even
better than many Christians?

One must rejoice if people who do not know Jesus Christ can work enthusiastically and unselfishly and be truthful and brotherly under all circumstances. As the Apostle Paul pointed out centuries ago: "When Gentiles who do not have the Law do instinctively the things of the Law . . .
they show the work of the Law written in their hearts, their conscience
bearing witness." Their guilt will become evident even to them "on the
day when, according to my gospel, God will judge the secrets of men
through Christ Jesus."[33] There is no doubt that a nation will be as strong
as its inhabitants are virtuous and conscientious. Nevertheless, if one has
read with attention the characteristics of true Christians described above,
one can observe important differences: the comparison between Christians and non-Christians must not be made in a superficial manner. First
of all, one must make certain that one is comparing non-Christians with
true Christians and not with pseudo-Christians of whom there are many,
as we have pointed out. Moreover, one must remember that the real Christian does not attain perfection beginning the day of his conversion. The
corrupt and lying "old man" continues to exist in him and even reappears
at times, but he disappears little by little in contact with the Word of God
and under the action of the Holy Spirit.[34] The essential thing is for the
believer to progress. He may have begun at a very low point when he met
Jesus Christ and opened his heart to him, and humanly speaking, he may
seem morally inferior to the pseudo-Christian. The pseudo-Christian,
however, lacks the regenerative power which has begun to transform the
life of the genuine Christian. Lives completely ruined, as men judge such
things, can be restored. This internal regeneration is also indispensable for
men who appear to be virtuous, because they too bear within themselves
the mortal stain of sin.

Moreover, in the very hard struggles which must be undertaken for
truth and brotherhood, it is not possible to conquer in one's own strength
alone, as the self-righteous nominal Christian might suppose. To restore
his inner strength the humble and faithful disciple of Christ can come continually to his God, the living God, Creator of heaven and earth, the

---

[33]Rom. 2:14-16.
[34]Eph. 4:20-24.

Master of history. He also has at his disposal spiritual weapons of which our materialistic world is ignorant.[35] Finally, the Christian who is nourished with the bread of life brings to the society where he lives something of inestimable worth and irreplaceable value: the blessing of God.

The blessing of God on the feeble life of a man or woman or a nation: Is this word devoid of significance for our materialistic and unbelieving world?

One must indeed have closed one's eyes not to have been struck by the historical examples of the children of Israel described above; one must be very short-sighted and possess a very feeble love of one's native land to scorn the civic virtues which multitudes of men and women who have been nourished with the bread of life could bring to it. The history which is unfolding before our eyes is there to prove it. Compare the national income per inhabitant of the different countries of the world. Then set up against it a map showing the distribution of the Bible. Among the most prosperous nations, those in which the national income per inhabitant is the highest, the following stand out: Switzerland, Sweden, the United States, Denmark, the Federal Republic of Germany, and Canada. In 1974 all of these countries had a gross national income per inhabitant of more than $6,000. These States are very different from each other. Some are vast and have abundant raw materials. Others are small and mountainous and possess extended uninhabitable zones endowed with little in the way of raw materials. Their political and economic regimes are also very different. But they have one feature in common. They are traditionally Protestant; the major share of their inhabitants join churches which have come from the Reformation; and the Bible is widely distributed. Today these countries are also ravaged by the spirit of material pleasure, dissolution, immorality, drugs, alcoholism, and other social scourges. Christianity is at times only a facade behind which there is no authentic and deep spiritual life. However, these nations still count an appreciable number of men and women solidly grounded on the Bible who have complete liberty to pray, act, and struggle without let-up against all forms of evil. Could the agreement between the presence of believers and the prosperity of the nations in which they dwell be the effect of simple chance? Economists have been much interested in this question. They ascertain that this is so and explain the connection between economic prosperity and a certain state of mind

---

[35]II Cor. 10:4. Cf. the discussion in *Le Maître* of the developments relative to the "arme absolue des Chrétiens."

which one finds in men nourished with the Bible.[36] Statesmen of the Third World must not indulge in illusions. If they wish the well-being of their people, it is not by industrialization, emphasis upon agriculture, and valuable institutional reforms alone that they will succeed. All of these costly efforts will remain incomplete so long as the government leaders do not have it on their hearts to distribute the bread of life abundantly and freely to their populations. The people who consume this spiritual food in suffecent quantity will be sheltered both from poverty and from the seduction of riches to which many men in the West have unfortunately succumbed.

Indeed the blessing of God is incarnate. It is linked to the presence, in all sectors of society, of believers who are receptive to the activity of Christ in their lives. Their witness and prayers constitute an imponderable but essential element for the moral health of the State. God hears and grants the prayers of his faithful ones.[37] The miracle of the multiplication of the loaves can be reproduced today. Both in periods of want and in periods of abundance spiritual strength is still more needed than physical strength. Scientific circles are aware of this as the development of psychosomatic medicine proves. Under these conditions, just as vitamins are indispensable for the health of the body so is the presence of Christians solidly grounded in Jesus Christ essential to bring a nation the material bread as well as the spiritual bread upon which its life depends. But in our time who understands this fundamental truth? Twenty centuries ago they crucified Jesus Christ who knew how to heal the incurably sick and to feed the famished crowds. Today doors are being closed to evangelical missionaries and Christians are being persecuted or ridiculed even where great poverty is the rule and where social plagues do great harm.

Nevertheless the day will come when humanity will cease to be stricken by famines, corruption, epidemics, and wars which result from its sin and rebellion against God. It will not be man's science and technology which will reestablish this golden age; rather it will be the Christ whom they crucified and who is returning soon as conqueror. Then he will assure bread in abundance for all, along with that inestimable good of which we must now speak: Peace.

---

[36]Octave Gélinier, *Morale de L'Entreprise et Destin de la Nation* (Edition Plon) esp. chaps. 8-10; Herbert Lüthy, *Le Passé Présent,* 2nd ed. (28 rue Comte Felix Gastaldi, Monaco Editions du Rocher). Most important is Alain Peyrefitte's recently published work *Le Mal Français* (Librairie Plon, 1977) with commentary in *ICHTHUS* (no. 7 Aug.-Sept., 1977). The address is 5, route des Acacias, 1227 Carouge-Geneva, Switzerland.

[37]On this subject read: Ps. 34:5-11; esp. v. 11; Ps. 66:16-20 and Ps. 144:12-15: "Blessed are the people whose God is the Lord."

PART TWO

PEACE

"Des silhouettes sont à terre, et c'est épars,
Nu, terrible, et le sang fume de toutes parts;
On entend un tumulte ailé qui se rapproche;
Et dans l'ombre, ici, là, sous l'arbre, sous la roche,
Dans les villes, au fond des bois, au pied des tours
Partout, on voit des morts. . . .

> — D'où . . . venez-vous vautours?"
> (Victor Hugo: Les années funestes.
> Départ et retour des régiments).[1]

Yes, "everywhere one sees dead bodies." And so it has been since the beginning of man, since the day Cain killed his brother Abel. Men talk about peace. Chiefs of State promise peace. But during the whole course of history they prepare for war out of prudence, and then, they wage it. People long for peace. But just let a bugle sound and an indomitable opposition looms up. Before men realize it they are launched on a frightful massacre. If one could conjure up in one's imagination on each parcel of land all those who have traversed it, there are very few places in this world where one would not see traces of blood. "The dead are everywhere. . . ."

In nature too there is an unceasing struggle for life. The bird feeds on insects. The great carnivores make all the animals of the forest tremble when they go on a hunt. Even in the waters of the vast oceans, the fish devour each other.

Is peace only a dream or a brief moment between two massacres? No. In the last days man will see the prophet's vision come true.

---

*[1] Silhouettes on the earth, scattered,/naked, frightful, and blood streaming from every direction;/One hears a winged tumult approaching;/And in the shade, here, there, under the tree, under the rock,/In the cities, in the depths of the forest, at the foot of towers/Everywhere, one sees dead bodies. . . . From where do you come vultures?

. . . He will judge between the nations,
And will render decisions for many peoples,
And they will hammer their swords into plowshares, and their
    spears into pruning hooks.
Nation will not lift up sword against nation,
And never again will they learn war.

(Isa. 2:1–4)

Thus, if one wishes to get out of the infernal cycle of war to bring real peace into this world one must, in order to discern the true remedies, concentrate on the causes of this continuous display of violence to which our humanity yields with a terrifying continuity.

Chapter 3

Analysis of the Reasons for Man's Failure to Establish a Lasting Peace

"I loved war too much," Louis XIV used to say at the end of a reign which began brilliantly but which ended in defeat and misery for the population. For a long time peace and war may have depended upon the good pleasure of the chiefs of State. For them, war was a sport, a grand hunting party, although at times it was more dangerous, since the hunter became, in his turn, the one sought. Louis XIV was not the only prince who loved war too much. Indeed, the exercise of power with all its military paraphernalia produces a sort of intoxication which easily seduces the human heart and in which the Christian discerns a Satanic action.

Thus the exercise of absolute power has succeeded in facilitating and encouraging war. Peace was rare when the bellicose ardor of tyrants had no bridle and when power was fragmented between numerous principalities. The most typical example of this is feudal Europe which lived in a permanent state of war between the lords of the epoch. Even with the establishment of the powerful States of antiquity, the emperors were always able to wage war on the frontiers of their empires and to harvest an abundance of glory. The warlike expeditions to the frontiers had to be carried on without ceasing. The emperors were able to participate personally in these expeditions. They would also send their best officers on them. Their victories lent prestige to their reign.

The love of war has not been the prerogative of princes only. The latter have always found generals, officers of all ranks, and soldiers to follow them on their most distant expeditions. "Lead us to the uttermost end of the earth . . .," cried the soldiers of Alexander the Great. These men did not march under constraint. They went to war voluntarily and even enthusiastically. They, too, loved war. They were ready to endure risk—death, defeat—in order to enjoy the intoxication of combat, the consideration and adulation which surrounds warriors, the glory and booty of victorious battles.

Thus, war seems to be the consequence of one of the natural passions of the human heart. There are some men, quiet and untroubled men, peace-makers, who can rise above their passions and subdue them. But there are also vicious men who look for opportunities to impose themselves by force.

Would peace be possible under these conditions only if a political regime allowed peace-loving men to hold power and—oh the irony of it!—to impose peace by force on violent men?

Democracy and peace

Such was the great hope of the French Revolution of 1789. It was necessary to overturn the monarchical institutions which gave power to kings who were too fond of war and too easily drew their unfortunate people into conflicts. Then peace and brotherhood would be able to flourish among all men beyond the frontiers.

The same hope also animated the combatants of the war of 1914-1918 who wanted to destroy the militaristic Germans who had instigated the war. It looked as if the bloody battles of that day would be the last. Victory was supposed to open an era of universal peace under the aegis of the League of Nations.

Today these illusions have vanished and men of this century seem to have lost all hope of peace. They live in secret terror of a great atomic destruction about which they prefer not to think.

What happened then?

First, note that democracy is an unusual form of government, which could not spread into all of Europe generally and even less throughout the world.[1] In France the Republic which was instituted in 1792 quickly degenerated into a regime of terror and anarchy which prepared the way for the Napoleonic Empire. Not until 1870 did the French succeed in setting up a truly democratic government.

In Italy and Germany the nineteenth century was more concerned with bringing about national unity than installing a true democracy. The First World War was kindled by wounded national pride which had been developing during the nineteenth and early twentieth centuries. The war had for its sequel a profound social malaise which was bound to lead sooner or later to the replacing of a poorly implanted democracy with fascist

---

[1] See *Le Maître*.

totalitarianism in Italy and national-socialist totalitarianism in Germany. After the Second World War another attempt to find democracies in these two countries seems to have been successful. The sufferings endured under the totalitarian regimes ought to contribute to the consolidation of the new form of government.

Spain and Portugal, which have lived for a long time under totalitarian regimes, have been trying since 1976 to establish a democracy. On the other hand, in Russia under the absolute monarchy of the czars, a strong official opposition has always been manifested against liberal ideas. The Communist government, which assumed power after the Revolution of 1917, has proved no better than that of the czars, having imposed its regime on all of Eastern Europe since the last world war.

It was in Northern Europe especially that democracies were set up in the course of the seventeenth, eighteenth, and nineteenth centuries. England, Sweden, Norway, Denmark, Belgium, the Netherlands, and Switzerland have had a long experience with democracy and, all but Switzerland, with the peculiarity of having retained at the same time an external monarchical framework.

Finally, if one adds to this list the United States of America and several independent countries of America, Africa, and Asia, which, for the most part, have emerged from British and French colonial empires, the enumeration of the States in which democracy seems solid is nearly complete. There is hope that Japan, which has been endeavoring to establish a democracy since the last war, may soon be included in this list.

In vast regions of Europe and the world numerous populations remain subject to totalitarian, dictatorial, or feudal political regimes which are very far from democracy. There is nothing astonishing about this situation. Statistics reveal that the areas of the world in which democracy is firmly implanted correspond almost exactly to that of the prosperous nations which knew how to choose a liberal economic regime, thereby assuring their optimal expansion. If one were to compare a map showing the countries where democracies with their liberal economies are thoroughly established with another map showing where the Bible is allowed free distribution, one would be struck by their similarity. The spread of democratic forms of government is therefore subordinated to the realization of psychological and spiritual conditions which do not yet exist in many States. Much more, the governments of these last countries are almost always vigorously opposed to all that could contribute to favoring the establishment of a liberal and democratic regime. The situation, humanly speaking, seems at an impasse for the time being.

Are democratic countries peaceful? Some might think so when they consider Switzerland and Sweden which have not known war for a long time. In the same way Denmark, Norway, and the Netherlands lived peacefully when they underwent the aggression of Nazi Germany in 1940. Democracy permits all opinions to be expressed. There are idealists who want peace at any price. There are also men and women who love peace—and that is the case with Christians—who seek to encourage a policy of peace but without, however, accepting imperalism under its various forms of international highway robbery. Then there are those labeled "hawks" who hold to a policy of firmness and accept the risk of war. Great powers endowed with democratic governments, like Great Britain and France after 1870, have proceeded in this way to the conquest of colonial empires, although they used for their military campaigns very few soldiers. These two countries also took part in the last two world wars which they had been drawn into by the system of world alliances to which they belonged. However, the study of the origins of the last two wars seems to indicate that these democratic countries entered the war only because they were attacked or provoked. Nevertheless, they will continue to be threatened permanently by the totalitarian dictatorial States whose leaders, like the monarchs of the past, risk loving war too much. The dictators begin campaigns at the slightest sign of weakness on the part of free nations because of their thirst for power or to reinforce their own internal government whose cohesion is only apparent.

The United States itself also took part in two world wars, as well as the war in Vietnam. The principal reason for America's involvement in Europe and Southeast Asia seems to have been to defend the liberty of the peoples of these areas. The Europeans were threatened first by German imperlialism and then by Nazi totalitarianism; the Asians, by communism. The Communists, like the Nazis, are skillful in masking reality and in using deceitful terminology. One must not be naive in the presence of their methods and propaganda, which insidiously intoxicate Western intellectuals. Just as the thief himself cries out "thief" in order to throw his pursuers off the trail, the Communist aggressor shouts "aggressor!"

Experience, therefore, demonstrates that democracies allow themselves to be drawn into war, especially where the great powers are concerned. Despite the peaceful tendencies which may be expressed within each of these nations, our world has not progressed toward peace in the twentieth century. A new and serious cause of conflict is apparent in the Middle East with the establishment of the State of Israel and the resulting Palestinian problem. The threat of a third world war exists once more. As in previous centuries, international relations remain very precarious. At a time when extraordinary scientific and technological progress has been realized in every domain, international peace is presently maintained only by a fragile "equilibrium of terror" among the great atomic powers.

The influence of religions: ancient paganism, Christianity, Islam

Religious and ideological concepts have a great influence for or against peace. Warriors historically have fought to the death, not only out of a thirst for conquest or a desire for booty, but because of a religious idea or ideal which intoxicated them into fanaticism. The pagan religions of antiquity are a perfect illustration. The pagan gods were peculiar to one city, to one nation, or even to one geographical region (plain, mountain, et cetera). According to the legends of the epoch, they were the ones who called the men of the city to war and led them in combat. An entire religious ceremonial surrounded the departure of the warriors. They were consecrated to their city-state, their people, and their gods by great feasts and thus prepared to sacrifice their lives. Their death was both an agreeable offering to the gods and an assurance of a happy entrance into an eternal world.

Like their worshipers, these pagan gods were generally bloodthirsty and warlike. They would be offered bloody sacrifices in exchange for their protection. The ramparts of the cities often contained a human victim empaled as an offering to the gods of the city-state to guarantee their effectiveness against the enemy!

The gods of ancient Greece and Rome were also warrior gods who idealized man with his penchants and vices. The worship of Mars was an abiding incentive to war just as the worship of Bacchus and Venus encouraged drunkenness and unchastity in the course of licentious festivities.

Therefore, it is not surprising that war was rampant in pagan antiquity as it was in Africa until the arrival of the Whites. It was encouraged by the peculiar character of the divinities and the religious patriotism which were closely connected with given people. This situation could change only with the development of great monotheistic religions and universalizing ideologies.

Belief in a single God necessarily entails the suppression of the absolute character of the city-state as the supreme good and the unique moral rule. If there is a conflict, it is the men who fight; it is no longer the gods. All the combatants have to give an account of their attitude before the same God. However, a distinction is established between believers and infidels.

The Jewish people, although monotheistic, were the first to wage incessant wars; they did so to conquer Palestine and then to defend it against its neighbors and the great Eastern empires. They retained, however, the hope of universal peace, the fruit of divine blessing which was foretold by the prophets. The reign of Solomon had given an indication of what this future full of hope might be. At that time the kings of the earth as well as the Queen of Sheba came to visit the king of Israel and to seek his wisdom. But this was only a brief rift in the clouds. According to prophecy, war, defeat, and deportation were going to sweep down upon the Hebrew people before they were finally dispersed throughout the world following their rejection of Jesus Christ.

The Christian faith in its original purity bore a radically new conception, different from all that had existed previously. So long as the divine revelation was limited to the Jewish people, the God of Israel could appear with traits comparable to the pagan gods since he was protecting a particular people. But the message of the prophets emphasized that the election of Israel was only a necessary step in the divine plan for the salvation of the entire world. Beginning with the first words concerning the call of Abraham, God had announced that this choice was made with a view to blessing all the nations of the world.

With Christ this radically new message is clearly stated. The gospel of free salvation, through faith in his sacrifice and resurrection, must be proclaimed to all nations. Christians are called to love their enemies and their neighbors, whoever they may be. Scattered throughout the entire earth, they should be the inspiration for a new ideal of peace and brotherhood among races. Christians can no longer engage in the patriotic wars which were sacred to the pagans. Nor should they consider the enemy a "beast" to be crushed or mistreated. They should recognize that all men have been created in God's image. Believers, especially, should demonstrate love and respect toward every human being, even though they are aware of the distinction between men who have acknowledged Jesus Christ as their Savior and Lord and those who continue to live in rebellion against God, voluntarily or unconsciously disregarding his commandments and the slavery of sin. Only believers understand the true Christian brotherhood which unites the disciples in love. Nevertheless, this brotherhood exists, and one of its functions is to proclaim the gospel to the lost and to prove to them the meaning of the love of Christ.

The reality unfortunately, is very far from such an ideal. An authentic Christian spirit of peace and brotherly love has had much difficulty penetrating our humanity which is so easily dragged into the ravages of war. In the various churches the old pagan spirit reappears frequently beneath an apparently Christian behavior and terminology. Thus, during the Middle Ages, in the period considered by some historians as the golden age of Christianity, wars between lords, princes, and Christian kings did not cease to rage. The alliance of church and state, which was prevalent in all of Western Europe and which the Protestant States themselves had difficulty avoiding, was nothing but the restoration of the spirit of the gods of the ancient city-state. Popes also took part in the conflicts, wearing at times a breastplate and bearing a sword, in order to fight as chiefs of State.

The peaceful spirit of Christ existed only in a small number of true Christians who were often obliged to find refuge in secrecy outside the too worldly official churches. Some unnoticed clandestine churches continued to survive in this way, silently, despite the persecutions and tortures of the Inquisition.[2]

Thus so-called Christian nations seem to be just as eager to instigate and carry on wars as other nations. They threw themselves into the great warlike expeditions of the Crusades. They left to conquer the Americas and then Africa and a part of Asia. They likewise fought savagely among themselves. Instead of the triumphal military parade after each victory of Roman emperors, they would sing the "Te Deum."

Islam, which is also monotheistic, likewise engaged in holy war. It even waged war much more systematically than the Christians. In fact, the Christians were not actually called to war by their faith but rather by a deviation from their religious views which, under cover of their religion, was allied to ancient paganism. With Islam the situation is different; in its case the doctrine itself encourages holy war. Participation in combat is one of the ways par excellence to please Allah and to assure entrance into heaven. One should not be astonished under these circumstances to find that the Muslims threw themselves with fanaticism into warlike expeditions and that they conquered large parts of the globe.

Are modern ideologies more conducive to peace than the religions?

We cannot examine here all the ideologies which have succeeded in gaining a certain number of more or less convinced followers, but only those which like the religions have had an impact on the masses and inspired the political life of the nations. These ideologies have appeared recently. First

---

[2]E.H. Broadbent, *L'Eglise ignorée* (Nyon, Switzerland: Ed. "Je Sème") and *l'Abrégé*, part II, chapter 3.

of all, there was rationalistic deism which, under the French Revolution, led to the worship of the Supreme Being, then fascism, national-socialism, and Marxism.

Nationalistic deism, which was instituted as the official religion under the French Revolution, is the fruit of various currents of thought which had been manifesting themselves for a long time in France. To begin with, there was the ideology of freemasonry which, going back to the Middle Ages, had been carried on clandestinely for several centuries in a monarchical state which was becoming more and more absolute. Freemasonry is not irreligious in principle. Some of its branches include sincere believers. But all reject the authoritarian clericalism of Roman Catholicism. They respect the procedures, questions, and requirements of human reason. The beautiful motto of the Revolution, "Liberty, Equality, Fraternity," is of Freemason origin. Sincere Christians can also subscribe to this motto provided that it is understood in a limited sense. The perversity of the natural heart of man does not permit putting it into practice unless one has been truly regenerated.[3]

The deism of Voltaire and the "philosophes" of the eighteenth century have some points in common with freemasonry. But in the case of the philosophes the accent is placed more and more on human reason which becomes an absolute, serving as a reference point on the scale of values. God is still recognized as the great architect of the universe, but the entire Christian revelation is rejected in favor of the light of intelligence and human reason. Thus, man becomes the center of the universe and the acting divinity.

The worship of the philosophes' Supreme Being, in spite of its beautiful ideal, has borne bitter fruit not only in France but throughout the world. Within France those who held this blind doctrine were the ones who led France toward the tragic regime of the Terror with its massacres.[4] Externally the armies of the Republic had to fight against all Europe. Murderous combats, involving large popular armies, were fought in the name of human brotherhood! Such perversion was certainly contrary to the initial ideal of the framers of this political theory. But one may say, in the light of biblical revelation, that Satan's rule is precisely this: to make a

---

[3]See the book by A. Kuen, *Il faut que vous naissiez de nouveau* (Vennes s/Lausanne: Ed. Ligue pour la lecture de la Bible).

[4]The Terror marked that period between the vote of the Law of the suspects, Sept. 5, 1793, and the fall of Robespierre, July 27, 1794. With the organization of the Revolutionary Tribunal, executions multiplied.

mockery of the good will of men who count on their own strength and do not seek the wisdom of God. One finds in fascist, national-socialist, and Marxist regimes a Satanic perversion similar to and paired with an apparently humanitarian ideal.

At first, fascism and national-socialism enjoyed a close affinity. Both grew up in opposition to the democracy which had been functioning for a short while under bad conditions in Italy and Germany after the First World War. The state of mind which allows democracy to function successfully, as we have previously emphasized, was no longer the dominant one in these countries. These nations voluntarily and freely gave the power to a leader who proposed to govern with authority according to the principles of a national-socialism. Initially such a regime brought certain benefits; public order was reestablished; trouble in the streets and strikes were suppressed; the entire nation was put back to work. Great public works were realized. National pride was adroitly flattered and elevated by sumptuous shows and extraordinary displays of flags and banners. The new regime was oriented toward an incredible exaltation of military virtues, having recourse to parades, moving spectacles with masses of men, tanks, and airplanes maneuvering with an impeccable precision, irridescent uniforms, and fiery speeches. All the enticements of the god Mars of pagan antiquity were displayed again.

Such regimes claimed to encourage national unity. They attained it not only by these enticements, but also by crushing all opposition. Those who were not in sympathy with their aims had to flee to foreign countries if they could, abandoning all their goods. When they did not succeed they were threatened, harassed, terrorized, and brutally torn from their homes to be locked up in the sinister concentration camps which are the disgrace of the twentieth century.

It is a strange spectacle to see reappear, in the very midst of the modern world, nations having all the nationalistic and exclusionary fervor of the ancient city-state. Their populations became infatuated with ideas which, to an outside viewer, seemed to come from another age, but which were put to work with all the refined techniques of propaganda. Behind this extreme nationalism, a semi-religious mystique began to be more and more visible with fascism modeling itself on ancient Rome.

With Nazism it was the Aryan race which was deified in a worship of the superman. The Satanic aspect of this mystique was manifested in broad daylight by the methodical persecution of the Jews. Of course, it was the Jews *qua* Jews at whom the Nazis were aiming, but, without suspecting it perhaps, it was God himself, his mark upon the earth that they wanted to efface. The Nazi ideology could not support the physical existence of a chosen people other than the Aryan race and another truly superior man such as Christ. This entire ideology collapsed after a few decades at the end of the Second World War leaving behind it millions of dead and immense regions devastated by the war.

The same myth of the superman and an analogous exaltation are found again today in the Communist world of Marxist-Leninist inspiration. Oddly enough Communist expositions display a new man of superior quality produced by Communist civilization. Surely this is the acme of human pride; it not only denies the existence of God by giving itself over to a militant atheism, but is also a sad parody of the new man in Christ. The biblical words become amazingly contemporary when confronted with Communism. They demonstrate with great wisdom that one may discern the good trees from the bad ones by their fruit. It is therefore by their fruit that one can recognize the quality of the new humanity produced by the Communist society founded on Marxist-Leninist ideology. No regime in the twentieth century has carried into effect so many massacres and deportations among the populations placed under its authority. No regime has had such numerous and full prisons. No regime has mistreated, exploited, and tortured its prisoners so frightfully as has the Communist regime. Such shameful and hideous fruit suffices to qualify this ideology, in spite of whatever fine social and scientific achievements it accomplishes. But what do we see in this respect? The USSR has managed to become a great industrial power. It was the first to send men into space. But today the United States has surpassed it in this domain also. On all other levels, industrial, agricultural, economic, the USSR is generally far from equaling or catching up with the United States with its liberal regime. The technical attainments of the USSR, therefore, are not superior to those of the free world and must not cause one to forget that the populations of the Communist countries live in a rather pronounced penury and, most of all, under a regime of policed terror. The members of the Communist party and the leaders themselves are perpetually in fear of denunciations by informers and arrests. The highest dignitaries have been made the objects of resounding condemnations. Even on the intellectual plane, the results are not encouraging. The young are indoctrinated in the name of a pseudo-scientific materialism in which all liberty of research and discussion is excluded and which is outmoded today on the scientific plane itself. Not being able to impose itself by persuasion and the value of its achievements, Marxist-Lenism continues to seek to dominate the entire world by force, subversion, and war.

Marxist-Leninist ideology still succeeds in making fanatics of enthusiasts in the same way that Nazism succeeded in making fanatics of the young who would charge against machine gun fire while crying "Heil Hitler" and would refuse blood transfusions with non-aryan blood! But it lost face as much within its borders as outside the Communist countries. It seems likely that free elections in these countries would immediately sweep away the Communist parties. The strength of these regimes is maintained only by an all-powerful secret police and an army to whom the most important resources of the State are channeled. In actual fact, therefore, Marxist ideology, like its predecessors, leads to bloody repressions on the internal plane and to a permanent menace against international peace.

Research of the sociologists

Only recently has war been analyzed as a peculiar phenomenon of the collective life of peoples. In France Gaston Bouthoul devoted himself to these studies and wrote several works on the subject. A French institute of polemology was founded in 1945.

These studies emphasized that the reasoned causes of war were only apparent causes. They are the occasion for breaking into armed conflict when a war psychosis has developed among nations. If this war psychosis did not exist, disagreements could arise without troubling the peace. Thus war appears as a sort of collective dementia which periodically grips nations and leads them to great massacres which they would certainly not carry out if they kept their senses.

These very lucid analyses have the merit of stressing one feature of the human heart which men today do not willingly admit: its murderous and destructive aspect. The fanfare, uniforms, patriotism, military honor, sense of sacrifice, and discipline—all that is normally respected, honored, and necessary in a nation—tend to mask the terrible and blind chain of events which leads men to frightful massacres. A strange psychological constraint takes possession of millions of men inducing them to perform acts they would never perform deliberately. Therefore, war resembles a sort of epidemic which periodically ravages humanity, like the plague or cholera. It is humanity itself that is sick. Is there a remedy?

Biblical revelation

At the close of this analysis of the diverse reasons which prevent peace from being established in a lasting manner on our earth, it is interesting to note that the conclusions of the best informed sociologists correspond to what is given in biblical revelation. Both affirm that the profound cause of war resides in the human heart.

From its first pages the Bible teaches that an initially good creation was corrupted by the revolt of man whom God had created free in order to obtain from him a loving service without constraint. This rebellion followed that of the celestial powers: Satan—also called Lucifer, or the bearer of light, a glorious and powerful angel—had preceded man in the revolt. The result was both an upheaval in the spiritual world, of which we have no knowledge except what the Bible tells us about the demoniacal powers, and the depravity of our world which we can see before our eyes. The visible consequences of man's revolt are described in the Bible as follows:

The suffering of the woman in childbirth is increased and she gives birth with pain. Her desire is for her husband but he dominates her. The soil is cursed. It produces thorns and thistles. It is by the sweat of his brow that man draws nourishment from the ground. Moreover, Cain does not think that he is his brother's keeper and kills Abel. From then on humanity, instead of being mutually responsible as God had intended, becomes murderous.[5]

Under these conditions it is not surprising that the following are acknowledged as facts which flow from the analyses made in the above paragraphs:

—The leaders of nations: sovereigns, kings, and emperors love war and its sinister glory. They drag their people into them.

—Democracy no longer carries peace with it. Certain peaceful groups, particularly of Christian origin, may express themselves freely, but their voice is rarely heard.

—All human religions are in fact bloodthirsty and lead normally to careless wars by which they glorify their combatants. The Christian faith constitutes an exception, but it can degenerate into a religion which quickly assumes the same sanguinary traits as other religions.

—Idealistic ideologies, however beautiful their principles, have also led to bloody massacres. The establishment of this fact leads to a second which is just as important: men who are inflamed by a great ideal corrupt it as soon as they want to bring it to pass by their own intelligence, because their hands and hearts have been perverted by sin. Thus they end by committing acts which are the very negation of the ideal for which they fight.

It seems clear, therefore, that the profound cause of war resides in the very heart of man. Is it possible to change it?

---

[5]Gen. 3:16-19; 4:8-16.

Chapter 4

Remedies for Avoiding War

There are three proposed remedies. Taking men as they are, violent and murderous, the first attempt was to impose peace on them by force. This was the peace which prevailed in the great empires of former days. Personal effort and collective discipline were also tried. Medieval Catholicism attempted this as does present-day Marxism. The third remedy is God's. Men are made new by grace through faith in the sacrifice of the Redeemer, his Son the Lord Jesus Christ.

The peace of the great empires: Babylon, Egypt, Rome

"Si vis pacem para bellum," the Romans said.[1] That was their wisdom in external and international politics. In this way they caused the Roman peace to rule over the civilized world. Their hold was harsh. But one must recognize that for eight centuries Rome knew no foreign invasion and the Roman Empire founded in 753 B.C. did not permanently disappear until the Turks captured Constantinople in 1453. The Roman Empire put such a deep mark on our world that the States of the West look upon it with nostalgia, frequently preserving its juridical principles as well as its political wisdom.

Other empires had caused a durable peace to reign within their frontiers. At the very moment the Roman Empire was being established the great and cruel Babylonian Empire, which had lasted for ten centuries, was disappearing in the East. It is the Egyptian Empire, however, which endured the longest period of time. Founded about 2700 B.C. it continued in almost the same manner for twenty centuries, that is, until 525 B.C. Like the Roman Empire, the Babylonian and Egyptian Empires maintained peace by force of arms. Later the Roman Empire was able to profit from the experience of its predecessors, just as we study the Roman Empire to

---

*[1] If you want peace, prepare for war.

learn lessons in government. These teachings, of the once great empires are very disappointing and pitiable on the human plane:

—Roman peace was sustained at the price of unceasing war on the ever-shifting frontiers of the empire. This rule was also true for the Babylonians and Egyptians. They never succeeded in achieving the world domination they needed to obtain a durable peace. The recruiting and permanent maintenance of powerful and constantly active armies were, therefore, the fundamental condition of a peace which was assured only at the center of the empire. The frontier provinces, on the contrary, experienced an ebb and flow of armies corresponding to the outcome of combat. Viewed from this angle the so-called Roman peace was only the Roman war reduced to a fundamental institution of the empire.

—Even in the interior, peace reigned only by terror. When Gaul was "pacified" by Julius Caesar, all who resisted were either massacred or reduced to the slavery of rowing on the galleys, working in the mines, and furnishing the necessary cheap moving force for the entire empire. It is estimated that the Gallic population, which reached about ten million inhabitants before the conquest, numbered no more than about a million inhabitants after the "pacification." These figures suffice to demonstrate the methods which assured the grandeur and peace of the empire.

—This policy of force could only be imposed for a time. All the great empires collapsed at the end of an apparently long time, but which is, nevertheless, a very short time compared with the history of humanity. One may wonder if the enforced peace, which was especially advantageous to the ruling classes, was really superior for the rank and file who were in bondage to the lawlessness which prevailed outside the "limes" in the midst of barbarous and free peoples.[2]

Peace by a voluntary constraint of human nature

In a certain sense medieval Christianity revived the ideal and even the institutions of the vanished Roman Empire; however, this was done by camouflaging them with a Christian terminology. The pope bears the title of "sovereign pontiff." This term is borrowed directly from the pagan religion of the ancient empire. But the comparison goes further: just as the Roman emperors were both religious and political leaders in the Roman world, so did the popes claim to reign both over the Church and all the kingdoms of the Christian world, realizing a universal domination.

---

*[2]This Latin word signifies the fortified line which marked the frontiers of the Roman Empire.

Moreover the entire history of the Middle Ages is characterized by struggles which the princes carried on to resist such political pretensions on the part of the papacy. But the claims of the popes to universal domination remained unchanged.

The popes sought to dominate the world in order to establish God's kingdom on earth. In fact Christ had spoken of God's Kingdom, stating that it was a purely spiritual reign awaiting his return. The popes, who called themselves the representatives of Christ on earth, wanted to correct and adapt the gospel. They kept Christ's terminology but without retaining the spirit. A dramatic misunderstanding developed in the course of the centuries. Instead of the peaceful reign of Christ, violence and terror held sway as in the worst hours of the Roman Empire. The Crusades and especially the Crusade against the Albigensians led to the massacre of tens of thousands of innocent victims, supposedly in the name of Christ.[3] At the time of the capture of Jerusalem, according to the account of the period, the Crusaders had blood up to their horses' knees. In the same way, at the siege of Béziers, the blood of the Christians who lived there flowed freely. The entire town with its 20,000 inhabitants—old men, women, and children included—was wiped out. On simple suppositions or denunciations the Inquisition made arbitrary arrests, tortured, or frightfully mutilated suspects. How could men who claimed to be Christians behave in this way? Men in Hitler's SS acted no differently, perpetuating the tradition of the Roman police. *Ben Hur* gives a striking illustration of Roman brutality. The Nazi regime lasted only twelve years. Imagine what it could have been if it had remained in power for centuries! Yet that is what happened in all the countries in which the Inquisition exercised control during the Middle Ages and up to the beginning of the contemporary era, particularly in unfortunate Spain. In *The Brothers Karamazov* Dostoyevsky describes very graphically the perversion to

---

[3]According to the Inquisition the Albigensians or Cathares were a Manichaean sect who combined certain Christian notions with the Persian teaching of the third century that there are two equal first principles, i.e., good and evil. The truth is that the original documents of the Albigensians were systematically destroyed by the Inquisition, so that only the Inquisition's accusations would remain. But a Cathare ritual was discovered in Lyon in 1887. The Albigensians were not Manichaeans but followed the rites of the early Church, rites based on the Holy Scriptures. They condemned the hierarchy, opulence, ceremonies, and morals of the Roman clergy. They may be considered forerunners of the Reformation. Pope Innocent III ordered a crusade against them in 1109 after which they were exterminated. The most brutal massacre was carried out in the town of Béziers in southwestern France where all the inhabitants including old men, women, and children, were murdered.

which medieval Catholicism led. The grand inquisitor exclaims in the course of the celebrated monologue addressed to the arrested Jesus:

> Thou didst desire man's free love, that he should follow Thee freely, enticed and taken captive by Thee. In place of the rigid ancient law, man must hereafter with free heart decide for himself what is good and what is evil, having only Thy image before him as his guide. But didst Thou not know he would at last reject even Thy image and Thy truth, if he is weighed down with the fearful burden of free choice? . . . We have corrected Thy work and founded it upon *miracle, mystery* and *authority.* And men rejoiced that they were again led like sheep, and that the terrible gift that had brought them such suffering, was, at last, lifted from their hearts. . . . We took from him Rome and the sword of Caesar, and proclaimed ourselves sole rulers of the earth.[4]

In addition to the Inquisition, which constituted its secret police, the papacy had at its disposal another weapon to assure its domination over all of Christendom. This was called excommunication. It was not a purely spiritual measure as one might suppose today in our modern societies which were able by revolution and civil war to extricate themselves from clerical domination. Excommunication was, on the contrary, a terrifying measure in a society entirely subject to the Catholic clergy. It placed the one thus censured outside of society. He was excluded from the human community like a savage beast or the lepers of ancient cities whom everybody was supposed to avoid and who lived far from the villages in caves. Until a few decades ago, free-thinking or Protestant teachers or public servants would meet with this treatment when they were assigned to little Breton villages which were still blindly submissive to their clergy. The inhabitants ostracized them and the merchants refused to sell them essential commodities! But that was only a very pale reflection of the excommunication of the olden days when there were no neighboring villages where one could go to stock up or no concerned governor to intervene in order to assure the respect of the laity.

Excommunication caused even kings and princes to tremble, for it released their peoples and their subordinates from any obedience to them.

Canossa recalls the power of the popes over the princes of this world in medieval Christendom. The German emperor, Henry IV, humiliated and

---

[4]Fyodor Mikhailovich Dostoyevski, *The Brothers Karamazov,* trans. by Constance Garnett (New York: Modern Library), pp 302-305.

half naked, waited a long time in the snow for Pope Gregory VII to deign to open the doors of the citadel for him.[5] Thus the papacy of the Middle Ages was indeed the heir of ancient Rome. Its power extended over all the kingdoms of the West through the princes who were subject to it, at least in theory, and by means of a hierarchical clergy like the imperial administrations of the old Roman Empire which controlled from within the action of kings. The secret police of the Inquisition, the Grand Order of the Dominicans, finally attained an almost total spiritual and material authority over the people. But the Inquisition never succeeded in completely enslaving men who were concerned about liberty. This is demonstrated by the fact that the papacy had to engage in incessant struggles to maintain its hold. Ultimately, the papacy lost its battle against liberty.

Therefore, in many respects the medieval papacy's attempt at worldwide domination resembled that of the Roman Empire. There are differences on the spiritual plane, however. While pagan antiquity took man as he was and tended to glorify him by his games, his military victories, his literature and his religion whose gods were in the image of men, the medieval world sought to improve man according to an ideal of Christian inspiration. Christ had declared that sinful man could not be regenerated except through a new birth obtained by the power of the Holy Spirit. But medieval Catholicism had set up an entire catalogue of mortal and venial sins to be avoided and virtues to be acquired at the price of meritorious efforts. Sins were discouraged by penalties, and virtues encouraged by rewards. Both were dispensed by the clergy, just as today the State distributes decorations and imposes punishments. Undeniably such a system can create discipline and emulation. By sheer effort, some men can lead apparently upright and worthy lives. But such lives run the risk of being only a facade behind which the passions of the carnal heart are simply held in check ready to surge at any moment. Frightful internal tensions can then appear in the hearts of men and women who live outwardly virtuous lives. This results in conscious or unconscious hypocrisy and lack of self-fulfillment. The same tensions existed in the society in which virtue was praised in principle but in which the grandees of the Church as of the State too often exhibited the most complete cynicism in the way they managed public affairs.

---

*[5]The pope, who had the power to humble the emperor, was resting at the palace of Canossa in northern Italy, en route to Augsburg where he planned to excommunicate Henry IV. Knowing that if he came as a penitent the pope would have to grant him absolution, Henry IV paid Gregory VII an unexpected visit. Thwarted in his plan, the pope still humbled the German emperor by making him wait three days in the snow before opening the door.

It is difficult to realize today how powerfully and methodically medieval Catholicism sought by sheer will and effort to create a new and supposedly Christian humanity and to bring about what it believed to be the kingdom of God on earth. The failure of medieval society is all the more significant. This entire totalitarian system finished by cracking. It did not succeed in achieving the worldwide domination of which it had dreamed. Its territorial expansion was halted by Muslim conquests which were stopped just in time.[6] Neither did it overcome its internal contradictions; in fact, it collapsed from within with the advent of the Reformation. Since then, just as the glory of the Roman Empire continues to haunt certain minds forgetful of its cruelties and injustices, so does medieval Christianity, with its hierarchy of virtues and sins, totalitarian structure, popes, bishops, and monastic orders with their human glory continue to produce dreams in the minds of those who trust in man and do not know the peace which only the living Christ can give. Today's Roman Catholicism remains so steeped in these medieval and totalitarian trappings that the efforts which have been made since the Second Vatican Council to readapt its doctrine and practice to the gospel and the modern world seem doomed to failure. Unless the Roman Church goes to the heart of the problem and rethinks the essential dogmas themselves, the changes will be purely formal and superficial. The mere idea of such a reform has already sufficed to shake all that secular edifice.

Today Marxist totalitarianism seizes upon the changes in Rome to attempt to extend its domination over the world and thus bring peace to men. It, too, seeks to realize a soviet paradise on earth. Marxist totalitarianism has dogmas which it imposes not only by official instruction given in all the Communist schools and universities and even in courses of various sorts at places of work, but also by a set of rewards and penalties going as far as a sentence in a concentration camp. It, too, has its secret police. It, too, gives itself a universal calling. The parallelism is extraordinary. One can only wonder how such a medieval structure can still exist in the twentieth century and seduce the masses. It is strange. It is also terrifying when one considers that all the modern means of science are at the disposition of the new inquisitors.

The failure of this system is certain. The signs are already in evidence. But what upheavals, what wars, what massacres will it entail before disappearing?

---

*6The spread of Islam was halted by Charles Martel at the battle of Poitiers, A.D. 732.

In a more discreet and even secret manner international freemasonry also attempted to bring about world peace by human means. It depended upon good will and reason. Although freemasonry was in a constant struggle with Roman clericalism, its principle of action was similar. This should not be surprising for its origin goes back to medieval Christianity. The Freemasons also built cathedrals but not being able to oppose the papacy openly they had to take refuge in secrecy. In fact, if they accepted the ideal of Christianity, they did not admit Roman Catholic totalitarianism. In Protestant countries freemasonry succeeded in developing complete harmony with the churches. In Catholic countries, however, it had to adopt a fighting attitude. Unfortunately this sometimes caused its anticlerical position to become secular and antireligious.

The Masonic ideal tends to produce a virtuous and free man. On the international plane it seeks world peace by reason, by fraternal contact between peoples and by conciliation and arbitration. This idea succeeded in becoming incarnate in the politics of democratic countries and in being conjoined with that of countries with a Protestant majority; the goal was to make peace prevail by negotiation, pacts, and an international organization of States. This organization, first, on the morrow of the armistice of 1918, took the form of the League of Nations—so tenaciously promoted by President Wilson—and, then, after the war of 1939-1945, of the United Nations.

A new conception of international relations was thus developed in the Western world following the Reformation, the French Revolution, and the expansion of republican and democratic political regimes which replaced the absolutist and feudal monarchies of the former regimes. International public law was strengthened and developed. Numerous international institutions were created: the Permanent Court of Arbitration was set up following the La Haye international conferences of 1899 and 1907; the Permanent Court of International Justice, was instituted by a decison of the Assembly of the League of Nations in December 1920; the League of Nations Pact was signed in 1919 and other international conventions were derived from it; the United Nations Pact was signed in San Francisco in 1949.

It cannot be a question here of retracing the entire history of these international organizations. They had the merit of bringing together the leaders and of giving all the States, great and small, the possibility of expressing their point of view. They also permitted the resolution of a certain number of conflicts between the States. For a few years one even managed to have the illusion that peace was finally going to reign over the earth through the application of international law. But these illusions were quickly dissipated scarcely a decade after the creation of the League of Nations. The authority of the international organization was not recognized by such great States as Japan, Italy, and Germany who resumed from 1930 to the Second World War the ancestral politics of national interest supported by force. Japan launched a long war of conquest in China. Italy invaded Ethiopia. Germany rearmed and, then, reoccupied the Ruhr. The League of Nations could do nothing effective to prevent it. And a few years later the Second World War spread throughout all the continents. . . .

Thus reason had succeeded no better than force in bringing about an organization among the nations and in causing peace to prevail. The fundamental defect of the League of Nations had been its failure to organize an international military force powerful enough to impose on the great States respect for common decisions. Economic sanctions adopted on the occasion of these conflicts proved to be just as ineffective as the disapproval of public opinion, an opinion which was divided by the skillful propaganda of the totalitarian States.

The United Nations, created in 1945 after the Second World War, followed the League of Nations. It attempted to avoid the pitfalls which had led the latter into failure and took measures beforehand expressly to provide for the use of an international army to prevent conflicts. This army was made up of contingents from the various participating nations. These United Nations troops intervened more or less successfully in certain conflicts: Korea, the Congo, and the Israeli-Arab conflict. But, like the League of Nations, the United Nations finds itself paralyzed by major conflicts between the great powers. Because of the right of veto in the heart of the Security Council the great powers are impotent in international incidents where irreducible divisions separate the States great or small. These oppositions are likely to lead to a new world war which would be all the more terrible since present-day armaments will cause ravages previously unknown.

In view of these somber perspectives, in the face of the hot spots of the Near East and Asia where any day the fatal spark may explode, one must recognize the failure of the extraordinary succession of conferences, meetings, and the various international organizations which have proliferated since the last world war for the greatest good of the international officials. Despite all of this window-dressing one is confronted again today by the fundamental and simple facts which have existed from the earliest times. Man is a wolf to man; hence, one must get used to the idea of permanent war. Happy again are those who live within the frontiers of a great power where the utmost possible respect for individual liberty and the human person prevails. Can men appreciate their good fortune and, when necessary, resolutely give their firm support to their government in the incessant struggles which it must carry on at the borders?

How right Bernard Shaw was not to be unduly impressed with the courage of the lion tamer who, inside the cage, was at least protected from other men. A well-fed lion has no cause to be malicious, for he has no ideal, no sect, no party, no nation—in short, no reason to destroy, except to eat.

This is indeed the crux of the problem of peace in the world. Neither force nor reason succeeded in establishing peace among nations. Neither the spiritual constraint of medieval Catholicism nor the totalitarian atheism of Marxism could change the heart of man. On the contrary, the results were the opposite of all the theoreticians' fine promises. It would suffice to ask—if one still could—those who lived in the jails and torture chambers of the inquisition of the Communist secret police.[7] If there were no other hope that these abortive attempts which stand out on humanity's road in search of peace, we might just as well give up and await like the Stoics or Epicureans, a final atomic conflagration.

One hope remains, however, which must be seriously examined.

Jesus Christ, the Prince of Peace, initiator of a new humanity

Many centuries ago, the ancient prophets of Israel were already looking beyond the land of Palestine where their small race lived. They greeted in advance a reign of peace upon this bloody earth. They announced the peaceful coming of the Prince of Peace who would be both the protector of Israel and the establisher of a world reign of peace and justice.

> For a child will be born to us, a son will be given to us;
> And the government will rest on his shoulders;
> And his name will be called Wonderful, Counselor, Mighty God,
> Eternal Father, Prince of Peace. . . .
> He is just and endowed with salvation . . . .
> And the bow of war will be cut off.
> And he will speak peace to the nations. . . .

---

[7]On this subject see R. Wurmbrand, *Mes Prisons avec Dieu* (Tournai, Belgium: Editions Casterman).

And he will arise and shepherd his flock
In the strength of the Lord. . . .
And this one will be our peace. . . .[8]
Then it will come about in that day
That the nations will resort to the root of Jesse,
Who will stand as a signal for the peoples;
And his resting place will be glorious.[9]
And he will judge between many peoples. . .;
Nations will not lift up sword against nation,
And never again will they train for war.[10]

Now this child was born in Bethlehem 20 centuries ago. A carpenter to the age of 30, he then had a brief three-year ministry in Palestine. Before his crucifixion, he said to the Roman governor Pilate, who asked him if he were the king of the Jews: "My Kingdom is not of this world." And since that time war has continued to ravage our earth. Could the Christians have been deceived, throughout the 20 centuries which have elapsed, in seeing in this Jesus, crucified under the jurisdiction of Pilate, the Prince of Peace announced by the prophets? That is what the leaders of the Jewish people of that day thought as well as all Judaism up until now. And nevertheless, on the whole earth, men of every tribe and race recognize Jesus Christ as their Savior and Lord. The Bible, the book which gives witness to Jesus Christ and permits knowledge of him in his innermost thoughts, is today distributed throughout the world by the millions. Those who read it as the Word of God affirm that the Holy Spirit acts in their lives as they depend on this inspired text and meditate on it day and night. When the good news of Jesus Christ is accepted by a youth, a man, or a woman, one sees alcoholics cease drinking, the fearful become confident and joyous, the timid become bold, thieves return their illicit gains, households become reconciled, violent men become gentle and peaceable. Yes truly, a new humanity, a better humanity, appears to be in invisible contact with the Crucified One.

Centuries have passed and peace does not reign on the earth, but the seed of the Word of God is being sown unobtrusively and irresistibly in the entire world, bearing as fruit the lives of regenerated men and women. This action is effected without constraint, freely. Contrary to medieval

---

[8]Isa. 9:5; Zech. 9:9-10; Mic. 5:3-4.
[9]Isa. 11:10.
[10]Mic. 4:3.

Catholicism, the faithful disciples of the Christ who constitute his true Church see, like their Master, that there is no constraint on those who receive the seed of life.[11] This seed must be accepted freely by receptive hearts in order to be able to grow and bear fruit.

Far from using the power of the State to impose their religion, his faithful disciples have, on the contrary, had to undergo persecutions from most of the governments in the course of the centuries. Today, again, they are welcomed either with indifference and weariness, or with incomprehension and mockery in many Western countries. They are imprisoned, tortured, pursued in the entire Communist world and in many of the States of the Third World. But through their ministry Christ is now present in the heart of all nations. The world is advancing therefore toward a radically new situation with respect to the history of mankind. This event is less spectacular than the landing of the first men on the moon. But, in view of the world's great disillusionment attested to by the slaughter of wars since the first days of humanity, there is in this an immense hope.

We see today, on the one hand, a silent expansion of true Christians in the world bearing the hope of universal peace in the name of Jesus Christ, and, on the other hand, a mute or open hostility of the States and of the majority of the people against these messengers of peace.

Just as humanity rejects today the One who could give it the daily bread it needs, in conformity with the conclusions of Part I of this work, in the same way it rejects the One who alone can bring it peace.

Jesus wept over Jerusalem twenty centuries ago, crying out: "If you had known in this day, even you, the things which make for peace! But now they have been hidden from your eyes."[12] A few days later the people of Jerusalem were going to demand his crucifixion. Then the city was destroyed by the Romans and the Jewish people were scattered throughout the world. Today the entire world is struck with the same blindness and refuses to see "the way of peace." It walks steadfastly toward atomic war and its aftermath of epidemics and famine. Very few seem to be aware of this somber tragedy. Neither the press, nor the radio, nor the television with its multitude of sources of information, allows one to grasp the present situation with enough perspective.

What will be the outcome of this tragedy? The Bible prophesies—and Christians await—the glorious return of Christ, the Prince of Peace, who will fulfill completely all the prophecies—alas—after war, epidemics, and

---

[11]*Le Maître,* part II, chap. 3.
[12]Luke 19:42.

famine have accomplished their devastation among our humanity who reject the Savior.

Then, when the King of Glory reigns in reality over a regenerated world whose inhabitants obey and love him freely, "never again will they train for war." Peace will spread throughout the entire world. Everywhere there will be water and food in abundance but also the justice and liberty with which we must now concern ourselves.[13]

---

[13]Rev. 21:5-27.

PART THREE

LIBERTY

"Attaché! dit le Loup; vous ne courez donc pas
Où vous voulez? Pas toujours, mais qu'importe?
Il importe si bien, que de tous vos repas
Je ne veux en aucune sorte;
Et ne voudrais pas même à ce prix un trésor.
Cela dit, maître Loup s'enfuit, et court encore."

("Le Loup et le Chien"—La Fontaine,
Livre 1, Fable 5.)[1]

As lovable La Fontaine expressed it so beautifully, liberty is worth more than bread, peace, and any treasure whatsoever. Every man worthy of the name is ready for any sacrifice to preserve or regain his liberty. This simple word has succeeded in exciting many nations in the course of history. With one bound they have broken their chains. We shall see it again tomorrow. The dictators, the new czars, know it well and they tremble.

If our Western society which presently enjoys liberty can no longer appreciate its savor, a few days without liberty will suffice to rediscover it in a hurry. The prisoners of the last war and the enslaved peoples under Hitlerian totalitarianism had the experience. Those who lived during these

---

[1]A collar! cried the starving wolf.
You cannot run at will?
What matters that the mastiff said,
I always eat my fill.
Though rich and regular your meals.
It matters much.
The dishes of a collared slave,
I would not touch.

(G. H. Clark)

somber years ought never tire of repeating to their children and their grandchildren what it means to lose one's freedom. The escapees from the world of concentration camps, which stretches behind the iron and bamboo curtains, are also there to recall the inestimable value of liberty.

A society which does not assure liberty to all its members is not a just society; there is no social justice without liberty. This is true not only for political liberty but also for economic liberty. Thus Lenin was right to emphasize that "in a society in which the working masses vegetate in misery, while a few handfuls of rich people know only how to be parasites, there can be no actual and genuine liberty."[2] Indeed, on the political as well as the economic plane, liberty for some to the detriment of others is insupportable, for it is a form of oligarchical dictatorship. Liberty for all implies civil equality and social justice for both the rich and the poor.

Under these conditions how does it happen that there are still so many countries in which liberty does not exist? Certainly there has been progress since the day Jean-Jacques Rousseau wrote that man "everywhere is in chains."[3] The 1789 revolution overturned many absolutisms and feudal systems. Its ideal of liberty, equality, and fraternity traversed the whole world. It still makes enslaved peoples thrill with hope.

But absolutism and feudal privileges have reappeared in the modern world under new names. A great fight for liberty must be undertaken once again not only by the peoples who are presently "in chains," but also by the inhabitants of the free world who too easily let themselves be enslaved by materialistic civilization. In order to carry on such a combat it is important to attack the problem by first distinguishing the causes of servitude.

---

[2]Lenin (1870-1924) was one of the great Marxist theoreticians, a leader of the 1905 revolution against the czars, and chief of the October Revolution of 1917.

[3]*Du Contrat social*, 1762.

Chapter 5

The Causes of Servitude

The causes of servitude are political, economic, and social.

Political causes

The most primitive as well as the simplest form of government is monarchy. The ancestral tribe has a chief whose power is not questioned. But often the chief can act only with the agreement of other notables joined together in a council or even of the entire assembled tribe. One passes thus from monarchy to aristocracy and then to democracy. According to this theoretical scheme the warriors of a monarchical tribe were probably "in chains" while those of the democratic tribe were free men. The reality is, in fact, not so simple. Indeed, even the most absolute tyrant must take into account what his subordinates think and try to win them over to his ideas. In the modern State he has available for this purpose all the resources of propaganda and psychological action, but he cannot persevere in a policy which runs completely counter to the majority of his subjects. The most he can do is to try to divide them in order to continue to reign. Contrariwise, in the democracies which possess the greatest respect for the liberty of each one of their citizens, emergency situations are always arising. Popular consultations are no longer possible and it is the chief alone who makes the paramount decisions. At such times it is not a question of minor decisions but of vital decisions upon which the very future of the nation and of the government depends, like that of declaring war, for example, or even of using atomic weapons.

Thus at certain times dictatorship and democracy resemble each other. The tyrant must take into account the opinion of his people and the chief of a democratic State sometimes has absolute power at his disposal. However, these two regimes differ greatly in the spirit which prevails on every rung of the ladder and which assures their functioning. In an authoritarian regime the primary virtue is fidelity to the chief who must be followed and obeyed under every circumstance. Everyone puts his trust in him and is thus relieved of the responsibility of understanding the fundamentals of national politics. In a certain sense this attitude is restful especially if a dictatorial regime replaces a poorly functioning democracy. The attractiveness of such regimes is explained partly by this psychological relaxation to which are added the immediate advantages of an authoritarian government: order, discipline, great public works, external politics of prestige, and the like. It is later that disillusionment will come with bitterness at having been seduced into abdicating the duties of reflection and critical observation which are incumbent upon every man worthy of the name. "Man is a thinking reed" (Pascal), and if he gives up thinking what else is left to him?[1]

In contrast to the seductive simplicity of authoritarian regimes, modern democracy calls for the establishment of complex institutions. Popular assemblies which make important decisions directly exist only in a few mountainous and not very populous cantons of the Helvetian Confederation. In spite of improved means of communication, democracy can no longer be carried on except in an indirect manner. Every citizen's capacity for initiative and the free exercise of all his civil rights must be guaranteed not only by a constitution which establishes a harmonious balance of the powers and assemblies, but also by a legislation and juridical systems which permit the effective exercise of each citizen's essential liberties while maintaining the discipline necessary to social life. This comprehensive view is difficult to conceive and to put into practice. One must not only understand democratic principles well and the teachings of comparative constitutional law, but one must also take into account the history and special character of each nation. That is why for a long time in France, owing to the memory of General Boulanger, it was not even possible to envisage a presidential regime.[2] Having these institutions set up with all the care in the world by competent men enamored of liberty is not sufficient to bring about a real democracy. A true democracy is a regime in which a sufficiently large portion of the people possess a sense of individual responsibility and a spirit of inquiry in opposition to the one of blind submission to a leader described above. Contrariwise, in all totalitarian forms of government, whatever they may be called, one sinks into a certain abdication

---

*[1]Blaise Pascal was a great mathematician, physicist, philosopher, and writer. He defended the Jansenists against the Jesuits in the *Provincial Letters* (1656-67) and was compiling material for an apology of the Christian religion when he died. The quotation is from the fragments which were published posthumously as the *Pensées*.

*[2]General Georges Boulanger (1837-1891) tried to use his popularity to overthrow the Republic, but the attempt ended in his flight and suicide.

of thinking and of an effective sense of political responsibility at all levels. People have managed to ridicule the term conscientious and level-headed citizen. Nevertheless, it is to such citizens that one must look for the spirit of democracy. An awakened and clear conscience is necessary to understand internal and international political situations; a free democracy cannot exist if it refuses to denounce evil, both attacks on the public good and the moral lapses of individuals.

Under these conditions it is easy to understand why democracy is constantly being threatened from within. As soon as the conscience of its citizens is lulled, as soon as their thinking becomes fuzzy, as soon as their virtue disappears, as soon as the internal constraint which they must impose upon themselves is eased, the entire political regime is endangered. This is how citizens of a free country sometimes grow weary of their liberty. They no longer see its glorious light. They are no longer disposed to pay its price. They forget that cruel constraints are going to be forced upon them, from without this time, by all the police machinery of an authoritarian State which will seek to entice them first in order to forge their chains all the more securely.

Such lassitude on the part of free men is particularly dangerous in countries where democracy is not solidly grounded. Some peoples have known how to carry on a brilliant fight for liberty. A case in point is France in 1789 when a great outburst united for a few hours the representatives of the Nobility, the Clergy, and the Third Estate.[3] However, the republican and democratic spirit had much difficulty gaining the upper hand in France because it was constantly striving against a tenacious, absolutistic current which was viewed sympathetically by a large sector of the population. This current is ready to re-emerge as soon as the political climate permits. It is old and permanent. It is the one which, with the support of a large group of the elite of an earlier time, led the French monarchy toward the absolutist regime of Louis XIV and his successors. The unspeakable drama of atrocious persecution which was initiated and maintained by the elite of this absolutist period against the Protestants and Jansenists[4] may

---

*[3]The Third Estate was that part of the nation under the "Ancient Régime" (before 1789) which belonged neither to the Nobility nor the Clergy. It included the land-holding peasantry.

*[4]The Jansenists were followers of Jansenius, a Dutch theologian and bishop of Ypres. They accepted the Augustinian doctrines of grace, free will, and predestination and placed much emphasis upon morality. Though persecuted by the Jesuits as heretics, the Jansenists, because of their sacramentarianism, did not consider separating from the Roman Catholic church to follow the Calvinists whom they resembled in other ways. In the eighteenth century they founded an independent Jansenist Church which today is affiliated with the Christian Catholic Church.

be likened to the heinous crimes of the Nazis. Life on the galleys differed little from that in concentration camps, and the attitude of Louis XIV's dragoons prefigured that of Hitler's SS. This regime had not only its ministers and its high and devoted functionaries, its *intendants* like the "sinister" Bâville who faithfully acquainted the royal court with his acts of cruelty, but it also had the applause of the vast majority of the Nobility and Clergy—not to mention the faithful of the cities and countrysides.[5] At the height of the eighteenth century, this spirit was still reigning when Voltaire, on the occasion of the Calas affair, succeeded in arousing those who had in them an elementary sense of justice.[6] And we find it again in the course of the nineteenth and twentieth centuries with the Restoration and its White Terror,[7] with Napoleon III,[8] the Third Republic,[9] the Dreyfus affair,[10] and in 1940 with the many partisans of Marshall Pétain's French State.[11] Curiously enough this same spirit is being manifested again today among men of the right as well as men of the left, who basically love absolute authority, one party, the leader, and all that this implies.

How is it that such a spirit, so ominous for a democracy, finds such favorable soil in France while in England, Holland, the Scandinavian countries, Switzerland, and the United States, the Fascists and Communists have never succeeded in assembling any but small minorities? If, once again, we divide the map of Western Europe between countries where the Bible is widely distributed, loved, and integrated into civic life, and those countries which are stamped with Roman Catholicism, we shall discover that France occupies a nuanced position. Although France has managed to escape the hold of integral Catholicism, thanks to her

---

[5]These royal functionaries of the sixteenth century were appointed to each province. They were directly responsible to the king and possessed financial, judicial, and police powers.

[6]Jean Calas was tortured to death, having been falsely accused of murdering his son to keep him from renouncing Protestantism. Voltaire was largely responsible for the rehabilitation of the family name.

[7]The royalists in the south of France were given this name during the first years of the Restoration (1815-16).

[8]Napoleon III, a nephew of Napoleon Bonaparte, wielded a despotic rule as emperor (1852-60).

[9]The Third Republic (1870-1940), which rarely came close to living up to its ideal, collapsed before the German offensive.

[10]Albert Dreyfus (1859-1935), a French officer and a Jew, unjustly accused of spying and condemned in 1894, was pardoned in 1899 and rehabilitated in 1906 after impassioned efforts on his behalf which divided the country into two camps.

[11]Marshall Pétain was the titular head of the authoritarian government which was established at Vichy during the German Occupation (1940-44).

Gallicanism, and although it was in France that liberal Catholicism developed and free thinking flourished, France remains more impregnated with the Catholic manner of thinking than she realizes. It is precisely this kind of outlook that leads Latin countries to waver between dictatorships of the right and Communist totalitarianism.

How is such a strong Catholic influence to be explained? First of all, there is Roman Catholicism's internal organization. Catholics have their religious life integrated into an absolute monarchy directed by the pope, with its local representatives in the person of bishops who also possess a hierarchical power over the parish priest and the faithful. The latter probably have an unconscious tendency to transpose this religious organization into political life, thinking that the structure which suits them in their religious relationships is likewise good on the level of the human city. Similarly Protestants, who possess a democratic and decentralized religious organization, would naturally tend to organize their city in a democratic manner.[12] But this influence of the ecclesiastical structure is not enough to explain the absolutist tendency of persons born in Catholicism but who are detached from it in practice: many exist in the Latin countries.

A second explanation completes the first. Instruction and general education inspired by Catholicism are conceived as a function of the same spirit of submission which is required of the faithful on the religious plane for the dogmas taught by the Roman hierarchy. Thus, at all levels of instruction, there is less to encourage young people to study the available original documents and to form their own opinions. Instead, they memorize the view expressed by their professors who have studied the documents and drawn from them conclusions in conformity with established dogmas. This method of teaching is found at all levels. Very heavy programs literally do not allow students time to study the basic documents for themselves, especially in history and literature. They can barely read a few brief extracts selected by their profesors which are far from giving an idea of the whole. The students are therefore obliged to trust their professors, accepting blindly their well-intentioned but sometimes false interpretations. The fact that this method, which might be justified in the lower grades, is perpetuated in the universities explains certain perfectly legitimate disputes. A salient feature worthy of note is that the Bible is approached in exactly this manner in the Roman missals and breviaries.

---

*[12]Their local assemblies elect councils of elders and send delegates who make up the regional courts, both national and international.

These missals and breviaries give only selected passages which are isolated from the context and whose sense may be profoundly distorted and adapted to Roman dogmas.

Therefore one understands why the inhabitants of a country whose university has been conceived according to Catholic methodology remain deeply marked by this methodology even when they are atheists. The inhabitants also feel at ease with Communism which offers them a hierarchy as well as dogmas to which they submit. Sainte-Beuve said: "As for what I believe, ask Rome."[13] The Catholic faithful submit to a further intellectual intimidation by going regularly to confession. This inevitably reaches the whole being including a person's intellectual and political opinions giving him habitual reflex action of servitude and resignation to a hierarchy which alone has the privilege of controlling thought.

On the other hand, in countries where the Reformation triumphed, young people are taught from childhood to examine things for themselves. On the religious level, the entire Bible is given to them as soon as they know how to read. They study it individually, in their family, at school, and at church. Always they learn to compare the different doctrines and traditions freely with the original biblical sources. The same method of thought is found in the schools and universities. The basic programs are lightened so as to permit the students to engage in as much personal research and reading as possible. Their critical spirit and their sense of responsibility are developed in this way. In certain universities, a democratic civic molding of character is given by the same method, for example, by organizing fictitious parliamentary sessions where the great questions of the day are presented from the point of view of the government, the majority, and the opposition.

Thus it is in the mind of men that liberty is forged or political servitude is prepared. This spirit is itself influenced by good or bad institutions. Political servitude will not be averted simply by adopting a liberal and democratic constitution. Teaching at all levels must be conceived in such a manner as to liberate the mind and to develop a sense of responsibility and initiative. The State can validly accomplish such a mission only if it is free and neutral with respect to every religious and philosophical doctrine. The separation of Church and State along with the doctrinal neutrality of the latter constitute essential pillars of a free society. This principle had much difficulty becoming established in the different States of the West. In

---

*[13]Charles-Auguste Sainte-Beuve (1804-69) is remembered chiefly as a literary critic and specialist in the history of French literature.

France, the Edict of Nantes marked one step along this painful road.[14] Unfortunately it was revoked a century after its proclamation.[15] In the eighteenth century the idea of religious neutrality made progress with Voltaire who, after having studied England and its tolerance in religious matters, advocated the suppression of the State religion.[16] Montesquieu expressed the same idea in the *Spirit of the Laws*.[17] This current of thought culminated in Louis XVI's 1787 Edict of Toleration in favor of the Protestants, and especially in the French Revolution's Declaration of the Rights of Man and their Law of the third Ventôse in the year 3 which specified that in the forms of worship no preference would be permitted.[18] Unfortunately, during the nineteenth century this beneficent principle of toleration was again thrust aside by the Republic itself. A concordat regime was maintained which gave considerable advantages to the Roman Catholics until the Law of 1905 reestablished the separation of Church and State.[19]

Once again, in almost all the other Latin countries, and even with the second John XXIII,[20] the papacy obtained the signing of concordats favoring Catholicism in one or several of the following manners:

—The recognition of Catholicism as the State religion, which carries with it the inclusion of religious ceremonies at official functions and the presence of the clergy at various public occasions. As a result, all the public means of expression: speeches, teaching, radio, television, etc. are utilized to propagate Catholicism and to give it a considerable publicity over the whole of the national territory to the exclusion of other beliefs.

—The State's assumption of financial responsibility for the payment not only of the previously cited ceremonies but especially of the salary for

---

*[14]The edict was proclaimed by Henry IV in 1598 to restore certain rights and privileges to the Huguenots.

*[15]The Revocation, signed in 1685 by Louis XIV, put an end to the advantages granted by Henry IV and began another period of severe Huguenot persecution.

*[16]*The English Letters* or *Lettres philosophiques*, published without authorization in 1734, constituted the first overt attack on the "Ancien Regime." Voltaire was obliged to find refuge outside Paris.

*[17]Montesquieu's celebrated *Spirit of the Laws* (1748) inspired the framers of the Constitution of the United States, chiefly in its advocacy of the separation of legislative, executive, and judicial powers.

*[18]Ventôse was the sixth month of the Republican calendar (Feb.-Mar.).

*[19]A concordat is an agreement between the pope and a government.

*[20]The first Pope John XXIII ruled from Avignon (1410-1415). He was deposed by the Council of Constance.

the entire secular and regular clergy as well as for the maintenance and construction of religious edifices, churches, monasteries, seminaries, and various institutions. Consequently there is a heavy burden for public and State finances. The heavy taxes which result from this are paid by the whole population including non-Catholics. This is profondly unjust. The Spaniard Professor Monroy, in a lecture delivered, June 8, 1969, in Geneva shortly before the pope's visit, estimated that such a burden is partly the cause of the precarious social situation of the Latin countries whose standard of living could be noticeably raised if a similar budget could be set apart each year for social work.

—The granting of various privileges in favor of the clergy and Catholics: juridical privileges for members of the clergy who may be sued only with the consent of the bishops, and access to certain State functions reserved for persons of the Catholic religion et cetera. . . . The result of these measures is to put all non-Catholics in a position of inferiority compared with Catholics, a fact which is an outrage to the dignity of the former as much as to their liberty.

It is interesting to ascertain that, in Communist governments, the doctrine and the Communist party enjoy privileges exactly comparable to those accorded Catholicism in the countries which recognize it as the State religion. Materialistic atheism benefits in such countries from all the power of State propaganda. It is officially taught in the schools and universities, preached on the radio, on the television, in the press, and in official speeches. It is the object of exhibitions and advertising campaigns. Similarly the various religions and other philosophical doctrines have practically no means of expression.

In opposition to the situation resulting from the signing of concordats with the papacy or the establishment of a regime of totalitarian Marxism, the State which wishes to assure the political liberty of its citizens practices a sincere neutrality with respect to all religions and philosophical ideas. It assures everyone a full liberty of expression, and is on the lookout to avoid all discrimination; the State also allows individuals to organize themselves as they think best and to provide for their own financial needs. The neutrality of the State guarantees the first and most important of public liberties, the liberty of thought and worship. The exercise of public liberties is characteristic of true democracies: liberty of thought and worship, liberty of expression, liberty of the press, liberty of meeting, of association, of work, and of going and coming, et cetera. Without these liberties political freedom is only an empty word. But the mere mention of them causes enslaved peoples to thrill with hope, particularly those of Eastern Europe who knew liberty a few decades ago.

Even in our Western countries one must still fight to gain certain liberties, medical liberty in particular. It is curious to note that a country like France which has been in the avant-garde in the struggle for political liberty and which has certainly seen the necessity for the neutrality of the state with respect to religious views, does not understand that one must act in the same way on the medical plane. The State ought to remain neutral with respect to the different schools of thought. For example, it cannot take the side of the allopaths[21] against the homeopaths[22] or inversely, and use public power to persecute those who hold the opposite medical doctrine. However, today in France, such intolerance is official. The State takes part in medical matters by its biased legislation on vaccination, by the regulations concerning the repayment of medical loans by Social Security, and by the manner in which the Medical Society is organized. It is not without interest to note that these last two sets of laws were established, one by a government with Communist participation and the other under Nazi occupation. But since then France has not discerned their harmfulness and has not repealed them. The holders of a medical view other than the official one are "persecuted" almost as the Protestants were under Louis XIV. They receive no honorariums and whatever they spend for medicines is not reimbursed. Children of those who oppose vaccination have been excluded from schools and family grants taken away from their parents. Adults who have not been vaccinated cannot pursue various professions. Legal proceedings are instituted against them. Doctors are no longer free; they live under the threat of being excluded arbitrarily from the Medical Society, thus preventing them from engaging in their profession. It seems like a dream to be recording such facts in the middle of the twentieth century.[23]

---

[21]Allopathy is that system of medical practice which aims to combat disease by the use of remedies producing effects different from those produced by the disease treated.

[22]Homeopathy, an art of curing founded on resemblances, teaches that disease is cured by remedies which produce on a healthy person effects similar to the symptoms of the complaint of the patient.

*[23]A better example for American readers of totalitarian trends in medicine is the fiasco of a few years back when the government tried to pressure everybody to take flu shots. The predicted epidemic did not occur and some people died from the shots. Fortunately many doctors saw this as a political move and advised against immunization. Although American doctors were not forced to follow the government's recommendation, the event illustrates very well the unfortunate consequencs to which bureaucratic interference can lead.

Here again the example of tolerance comes to us from England. After having been the first country to require vaccination, it was also the first to recognize the medical and psychological dangers of its practice. It reestablished vaccinal freedom. A number of countries have already followed suit. France, unfortunately, still perseveres for the moment in the opposite direction by multiplying the number of obligatory vaccinations and stifling the voices of the oppressed minorities.

Finally it is advisable to emphasize that even in countries where men's fundamental liberties are officially recognized a sort of administrative tyranny can be set up. Modern States have a tendency to adopt legislation and especially regulations for the application of laws which can be particularly complex. Only specialists are able to understand all their subtleties by remaining in close contact with the administrators. The judicial principle which states that no one can be ignorant of the law then becomes unworkable. The conditions of their application depend above all on the good will of the officials who have the responsibility for applying these laws. These officials can always find their "subjects" at fault on some point in spite of the subject's good faith. Thus arbitrariness reappears under the cover of the laws.

In conclusion, political servitude can be developed even within free institutions if there is not a large enough body of citizens capable of reacting continuously with a clear vision and a profound thirst for liberty. How to set up such institutions and above all how to have such citizens is the basic problem to which we shall have to return.[24]

Economic causes

People can also be in chains on the economic level. The ancient Greek city-states used to be proud of their democratic institutions and of the liberty of their citizens. But their material existence was generally assured by a multitude of slaves who were deprived of all rights and considered and treated as beasts. It was the same with the Roman Republic as soon as victorious wars had increased its power, raised its standard of living, and furnished slaves.

Feudal society also submitted the people to a hard servitude. Artisans and peasants were tied to their trade and to their land by means of guilds and serfdom. Even slavery was still in force until the nineteenth century.

---

[24]See further on in chapter 2, "The Conquest of Liberty."

The treatment of the Blacks at the time they were headed for North and South America is a disgrace to the West.[25]

Thus the people were chained to their work with no possibility of discussing the conditions and modes of payment which were regulated in a rigid manner, without benefiting from vacations beyond a few days for religious feasts and without being able to get away to look elsewhere for work. Economic conditions were generally very precarious following epidemics, insufficiency of cattle, natural disasters, uncertain means of communication, and devastations due to incessant wars. Thus the people scarcely possessed the bare minimum and submitted to the work-yoke in all its harshness.

These conditions lasted for centuries in all European countries up to the moment the feudal regime began to crack. The industrial revolution often preceded and accelerated political transformations. These changes were carried out either by a progressive evolution as in England or by a profound revolutionary conflagration as in France in 1789 and in Russia in 1917.

In Western countries, the economic revolution, along with the political evolution, also moved in the direction of liberty. Economists conceived the doctrine of economic liberalism known as laissez faire capitalism. They had confidence that the automatic regulation of prices by the law of supply and demand would guide production in the best interests of consumers.

This doctrine greatly facilitated economic changes: guild rules were abrogated; town dues and domestic tariff-walls were abolished; new factories could be freely built; peasants who were liberated from servitude left their non-income-producing lands to go to work in industry. Commercial exchange was multiplied within each country as among the nations. National and international division of labor was brought about permitting a considerable lowering of prices and a correlative increase in consumption. In this way the nations of the West were enriched. They were no longer at the mercy of famines. Their standard of living was raised bringing with it a considerable improvement in hygiene and public health.

But there are two sides to every coin. It took time for the governments and the economists who advised them to perceive that total noninterference of the State in economic life also produced excesses. The monopo-

---

[25]See especially the documents on display in the Marine Museum in Nantes.

ly of riches was one excess for which it was urgent to provide a remedy without impeding the functioning of the market economy and the law of supply and demand. In this way legislation was promulgated against monopolies, the United States anti-trust legislation being the most typical for maintaining free competition and initiative for all. On the agricultural level, the appropriation of lands by those who cultivate them was encouraged; this involved the dividing up of the great estates. In some countries like France, the division of the lands was carried out in a drastic manner as a result, first of the Revolution of 1789 and then of the civil legislation on inheritance. Now it is necessary to regroup arable regions and small fragments of land to obtain units large enough for profitable cultivation. Finally a comprehensive labor legislation was instituted to assure workers of humane working conditions: limitation of the number of hours of work per day, control of workshop hygiene, union rights, right to strike, social security, and shares.

Today it is no longer so much upon rights that we need to insist as upon duties, for the latter are woefully misunderstood. Thus the perfectly legitimate right to strike can give rise to intolerable abuses when it is exercised in public services (transport, communication, water, gas, electricity, and hospitals, for example) which by definition must not be interrupted. In these domains different means can be used to permit workers to make their voices heard without interferring with public services.

The liberty of all citizens on the economic level is manifested by a general rise in the standard of living, by the possibility of all to acquire property—especially that of lodging—and by the establishment of savings sufficient to shelter families from the consequences of a temporary halting or shutting down of work. This condition comes close to being realized in countries like the United States, Switzerland, and Sweden where workmen and farmers have their own homes, automobiles, and bank accounts. We must consider carefully the reasons which prevented other nations, equally well endowed with natural resources, from attaining a similar prosperity and liberty.

Western Europe was ravaged several times by international wars and revolutions while the United States had only the Civil War which destroyed their own territory. Europe remained divided into nations practicing protective customs duties until the creation of the European Economic Community by the Treaty of Rome, March 25, 1957. The goal of this community was the formation of a common market. Prior to this, industry had not been able to develop vast markets and to organize on a large enough scale to allow the kind of division of labor which permits the lowering of prices. Besides, economic liberty within the States was too often stymied by regulations that failed to recognize automatic price control and hindered its functioning. An individualistic and overly cautious state of mind resulted which contrasted with the dynamism of the American industrialist. But fortunately, an evolution of organizations and mentalities has been underway ever since freedom of exchange and circulation was established in the European Economic Community, presently known as the "Europe des neuf."[26] The outcome could be a renewal of Western Europe if the people who comprise this group would not limit themselves only to economic considerations but would decide at the same time to struggle victoriously against all that threatens their physical and moral well-being: alcoholism, drugs, sexual license, and occultism. What is needed is the rediscovery of a genuine Christian faith.

In Russia and other Communist countries attempts at economic liberalization were halted the moment the Communists assumed power by the establishment of a totalitarian regime which was just as political as it was economic. The economic shackles of the medieval feudal system were in evidence once more under different names. The adaptation of production to consumption was effected in an authoritarian manner by a wholesale leveling which resulted in adjustments and directions much less precise than automatic price control. Strikes were forbidden. The right to organize labor-unions did not exist. Workmen could not seek employment freely. Their activities and their moves were generally controlled by a slip of paper analogous to the old "livret de travail" which existed in France at the beginning of the nineteenth century and whose abolition was hailed as a victory by workmen. Individual initiative was hampered at every level and even penalized by the secret police. As a consequence the economy lacked dynamism and the standard of living of the masses remained abnormally low. Much more, by the expediency of rationing, the economy became a way of exerting pressure on individuals as well as producers. Political servitude was cemented by economic subjugation.

Social causes

Servitude develops even on the social plane in various manners. It is im-

---

[26]Since 1973 the C.E.E., which was created by the treaty of Rome, 25 March 1957, has been made up of the following nine members: Federal Republic of Germany, Belgium, Denmark, France, Great Britain, Ireland, Italy, Luxembourg, the Netherlands.

portant to be particularly vigilant, in our theoretically free societies, ready to oppose constraints which reappear unofficially either due to differences in race, class, or life style or in connection with the public means of expression.

Constraints due to differences in race, class, and life style

We shall not be concerned here with racial or social distinctions sanctioned by the laws. Questions of that sort might arise in the political domain. For example, when India introduced a caste of pariahs into its legal structure, the liberation of this lowest class of Indians was a political matter. But the day this legislation was repealed the constraints and prejudices which lingered on because of the old caste spirit became a social concern. In practice, therefore, distinctions could be maintained which the law had abolished. This is often the case in our modern societies. In France especially the nobility was legally abolished along with the royalty. But some people continue to attach a certain value to titles of nobility.

Similar sentiments can arise on many occasions; between manual workers and intellectuals, city-dwellers and country-dwellers, rich and poor, leaders and followers, et cetera. A situation independent of our own will can thus become a barrier for us, a hindrance which closes doors, isolates and imprisons us within a certain milieu. In this case the chains are no longer obvious, but they do exist internally and psychologically. They can be heavy to bear for those who must support their weight. They are still heavier when philosophical and political doctrines raise barriers between men and give them a permanent character. It is thus that the Marxist doctrine of class struggle postulates the existence of clearly defined social classes and from this fact tends to raise barriers between men even in places where they do not actually exist. Much more, it gives the proletariat a redemptive role which leads to scorn for all who do not form a part of the chosen class. The Communist leaders pursued similar doctrines when, at the end of the last world war, they practiced a systematic policy of extermination of the former social elite in every country in which their armies were victorious.

Racial prejudices like social prejudices are also the origin of many lamentable troubles and suppressions. Both seem to arise from natural tendencies of the human heart. They are therefore particularly difficult to combat. A social pressure opposed to these prejudices can certainly suppress them for a while. But they reappear very quickly. What's bred in the bone will come out in the flesh. This is what one sees in the United States, particularly where the majority remain theoretically devoted to the spirit of Christianity which leads one not to discriminate between men but to consider all of them as brothers and to love them as a result. But when a deep and vital faith is not constantly renewing that spirit in the leaders as well as in the humblest citizens, racist attitudes quickly reappear. The War of Secession took place in the last century to abolish the slavery of the Blacks and to give them citizenship. But at present, more than a century after this war, a distressing racial problem still exists not so much because of the institutions, but because of the state of mind that prevails in the heart of the population. Many nominal Christians, active members of churches, tragically forget the person and mind of Christ when a Black wishes to live in their neighborhood or in their house.

> He has no stately form or majesty
> That we should look upon him,
> Nor appearance that we should be attracted to him.
> He was despised and forsaken of men,
> A man of sorrows, and acquainted with grief;
> And like one from whom men hide their face,
> He was despised, and we did not esteem him.
>
> (Isa. 53:2-3)

Racial differences are facts of nature which one would be wrong not to take into account. To be unaware of them would be as great an error as racism.

Without a spirit of love it is not possible to find solutions to this problem, solutions which would face the issues squarely and at the same time encourage a conduct which would assure the human dignity of all and esteem for one another.

If today's Christians forget that the Blacks, the Jews, the poor, the forsaken, the unfortunate of all sorts are brothers whom one must rescue, help, and, most of all, love in order to restore to them their sense of human dignity, who can do it in their place? Only love of Christ is transmitted and spread by means of his humble disciples who are thus really the salt of the earth and the light of the world. But what if the salt loses its savor? "It is good for nothing any more except to be thrown out and trampled under foot by men."[27]

Elsewhere there are not only racial tensions between Blacks and Whites.

---

[27] Matt. 5:13.

In Paris before 1940 cries against the "wops" would alternate with "France for the French." At the same time the "Aryans" were excluding Jews from their national community with the abominable procedures we know. Likewise, in our cities and even in our transportation systems there are groups who find it difficult to exist side by side without annoying one another, even though they are less differentiated than the racial communities: smokers and non-smokers, for example. There are sections reserved on trains and planes for each of these groups and nobody sees this as a form of segregation. Many non-smokers are vexed and misunderstood by the smokers who happen to be in the majority, and they suffer without objecting too strenuously. But since disputes are fashionable and since often only those who cry the loudest seem to be heard, should such people form a union and add weight to their accusations by demonstrations? Cannot all the citizens of a country accept the fact that in any human society whatsoever there will necessarily be great religious, racial, and social diversity and that a harmonious group-life requires respect for and knowledge of these differences between men?

There again love could change everything. It permits one to regard each situation in a different manner, with a new spirit which Christ places in all those who ask him for it. This spirit would allow one to take into account natural differences by integrating them in one great flash of understanding, mutual esteem, and love and by expressing this new relationship in daily life as well as in institutions. Today this spirit and these new relationships appear only in an uncertain and occasional manner. They are harbingers of a human society regenerated from within which will be manifested when Christ returns, glorious, to reign upon this earth. At present men who are open to this revolutionary manner of seeing are too rare.

Technological dictatorship in modern society

Citizens of ancient cities where democracy reigned, could express themselves publicly when the population met in the public square, the Roman forum, to tackle the great problems of State. Then all one needed to be heard was a good voice. The limits of their world scarcely extended beyond the walls of their city. They were unaware of the very existence of the sparse populations in the forest or large prairies which used to cover the regions where now the most active cities of the modern world exist.

Today, we can be informed every day by radio, television, and the press of what is happening throughout the world. We are called to reflect upon all sorts of political, economic, social, philosophical, and religious problems. This thinking, matured and enlightened by contact with the news, remains indispensable to the proper functioning of a democracy. The political choices that are made in a country at the time of the election of a president or of the members of a representative national assembly, for example, sometimes have repercussions in all the countries of the globe.

But our liberty is affected if our information is not good and if we cannot know the various ideas pertaining to such and such a problem, just as much as if we are not able to express our own opinions. This is exactly what is happening today on a vast scale in our Western democracies where, if we are careless, not a political dictatorship, but a technological one may prevail, thanks to the bias of the media.

In many countries radio and television are state monopolies. But broadcasting stations situated beyond the national frontiers can also reach the listeners. The latter, therefore, have the possibility of evaluating the national broadcasting stations by comparing their news with that coming from foreign countries. This competition is salutary and certainly contributes to attempting the risks of technological dictatorship and monolithism. This competition will improve with technical progress which permits a better reception of broadcasts from the entire world with small transistor radios. Even telecasts from other countries, which are often a state monopoly, can be received locally and worldwide through retransmission by satellites.

But as long as national or commercial broadcasts are not open to different currents of thoughts, to diverse political, philosophical, and religious groups, and even to individuals who have ideas to express, liberty will not be complete. Therefore it is of primary importance for a country concerned with liberty to have a law requiring freedom of speech on radio and television. Access to these means of expression must depend not on the greater or lesser breadth of view of a director or departmental head, but on public regulations which are acceptable to all and which make it possible for minorities to give their individual viewpoints. Each shade of opinion might have at its disposal a certain time at the radio or on television screens, just as, for example, this is worked out in France at the time of the presidential elections.

Access to the press poses a different problem. There is no State monopoly in this sector. But the launching of a press enterprise requires tremendous capital and the big newspapers with different biases hold their positions solidly. Even the circulation of a small newspaper of a few pages involves high costs. Besides, the opinions which are expressed in it are scarcely noticed because of the advertising which captures the reader's attention by announcements, displays, and all kinds of pictures. Thus the voice of the weak and isolated is very quickly suppressed. How to break this servitude? One must stretch the imagination to come up with original solutions. Here again, as with radio and television, carefully worked out legislation which takes into account the imperative of liberty for all should permit the restoration of a true freedom of expression.

For the moment it would seem that such solutions are far from being realized even in the Western world where one would expect the love of liberty to exert a great force. After all, one speaks of the free world in opposition to the Communist world in which the essential human liberties are openly scorned. How strange it is to see servitude reappearing on the whole earth in the most subtle manner among men who in their innermost being are enamored of liberty!

All of this reflection on the causes of servitude ends with the following disappointing affirmations: the fight for liberty must be constantly renewed. When a victory has been won, it remains precarious. New bonds are always reappearing either openly or in an insidious manner just as weeds pulled from a lawn grow back more quickly than the grass. New battles must be constantly fought. Freedom's adversaries are all the more difficult to subdue because they live in the very heart of man.

It is an old story whose explanation is found in the Bible. Ever since man's rebellion against God the human condition can be understood only in terms of his bondage to sin. Since then the quest for liberty assumes vast dimensions not only on the material plane but also in the very center of spiritual life.

Chapter 6

The Conquest of Liberty

"The capture of the Bastille weapons in hand. . . ." So cried the French revolutionists of the eighteenth century as they protested against imprisonment merely by orders under the king's seal or reason of State. There are still many Bastilles to be stormed in our world of the twentieth century with its more effective techniques extended over much larger territories. Perhaps we shall soon see nations oppressed enough to rise again, for the flame of freedom is never extinguished in man's heart. The Hungarian uprising gave an admirable example of what a nation can do without arms against modern armored vehicles. To be sure the rebellion was crushed. But Hungary is a vast plain which facilitates the deploying of tanks. Moreover, the Hungarians were alone. What will the Russian Communists do the day a vast popular uprising embraces not only Hungary but also Czechoslovakia and Rumania with their mountains so ideal for guerrilla warfare when patriots enamored of liberty rise up in their very own country and interrupt the means of communication, when the prisoners of Siberia crush their jailors? That great day is perhaps closer than many think. The immense Soviet and Chinese Empires could collapse in almost no time at all like a castle of cards, for they are founded not on justice, but terror.

Such a collapse has already been seen in Indonesia where the Communists, who had every advantage, were hunted down in a few days. But without even being foreseen and organized similar popular uprisings seem inevitable. Some unworthy governments have heaped up against themselves such hatred, such unshakable opposition, that a popular explosion is necessary to establish equilibrium. That was the case in the France of 1789 where monarchical absolutism had been tragically oppressing France for a century. In Russia in 1917 the czarist regime was exploded in the same way. Tomorrow there will again be other outbursts wherever totalitarianism reigns.

What then? The drama of Russia was to see one absolutism collapse only to be succeeded by another even harsher one. Everything began again because in 1917 a Lenin was found to seize the revolutionary opportunity and to divert the course of events in the direction of a new slavery. All would have been different if another team of men with character and enamored of liberty had been there to grasp the opportunity to oppose this monopoly of revolutionary enthusiasm. They could have guided the Russian people toward the liberty for which they were hungering after centuries of servitude.

The conquest of political liberty, first of all, but of economic and social liberty as well, requires, therefore, the human, intellectual, and spiritual formation of as solid an extensive and elite as possible, adequate under all circumstances to seize power and to retain it. Men who suddenly find themselves in control must know exactly what measures are necessary to restore lasting liberty and to defend it against every totalitarian attempt.

It is important to be very precise about such a formation and to promote it.

Apprenticeship in the techniques of liberty

In every country an elite group of men and women should be busy learning and perfecting the techniques of liberty. Such an effort is necessary in the free world for we saw in the preceding chapter that liberty is always being threatened by revolutionary enterprises on the social and technical level, if not on the political one. This effort is still more indispensable in countries where totalitarianism reigns. In those places this work cannot be accomplished in broad daylight. These teams must be patient and not become weary. Dictators do not willingly give up power. But if one day the dictator falls following a revolutionary uprising of the enslaved population or a foreign war, it will be important then for political teams to be ready to assume the responsibility of power. That will require political teams with virtuous men, intelligent and dedicated, and trained by a persevering effort in adversity.

Like other disciplines, the political sciences form the object of studies on the international level. Professors, writers, jurists, and economists from different countries of the world contribute to its progress, its research, its questions. A vast effort of thought and reflection ought thus to be pursued by all persons having responsibility for teaching, training, and political action. Reviews, technical books, articles in the public press and round tables on radio and television, and speeches of all sorts express this effort which is spread from country to country by extensive translation and cultural exchange.

It is by relying on this work that teams can be formed to assume political responsibility for implanting liberty or preserving it in their own country. National teams must be capable of adapting to their country institutions which have been tested abroad, of translating into national realities the principles of liberty in political, economic, and social matters. This is an exciting work with an immense outreach. How disappointing it is to discover often that the political parties of democratic countries have no idea of this and betray their fundamental vocation!

On these teams there may be specialists of various sorts. Some are more competent in the area of history. Others go deeply into legal data in the area of the constitution and public law. Still others study social, racial, and ecclesiastical relationships. . . . All must be animated not only by a profound love of liberty but also by a true human understanding, a compassion for the problems and situation of the less favored, of those whose liberty is comprised or threatened by the evolution of the modern world.

In this way a clear and precise plan of action is ready to be adapted to all situations and to mold new institutions of a free, just, prosperous, and fraternal society. It can be briefly summed up as follows:

—A constitution assuring the balance of legislative, executive, and judiciary powers. A study of comparative constitutional law, which goes beyond the limits of the present work, appraises the value of different proposals adopted in this connection. It is naturally up to the national teams to adapt these institutions to the historical and ethnical situations in their own countries, federal formulas being those which best guarantee national unity in liberty and diversity.

—A universal majority suffrage permitting the participation of a stable majority qualified to govern. Similarly, constitutional guarantees could be provided to permit all political parties and minorities, in particular, to express themselves by means of the media.

—The effective guarantee of physical and spiritual integrity for everyone. This principle bears three very important consequencs. First of all, a true State neutrality must be realized in every domain. That does not mean that responsible politicians are unaware of the importance of religious and philosophical doctrines or of medicine. But the State must allow each one of them to be expressed freely and independently if it wishes to respect the various spiritual families or schools of thought which necessarily coexist in our human societies. Placed in competition in this manner, religions, philosophies, and medical conceptions will not be put aside but will, on the contrary, be given a stimulus when they correspond to a real force. Those which existed only as a matter of form with the support of a political regime will find again their true place and perhaps a different life.

Next, it is necessary to adopt legislation inspired by the principles of the celebrated English "habeas corpus" law which would eliminate all arbitrariness with respect to persons, in particular those who are suspected of crimes and offenses but who may be perfectly innocent and must be treated as such until a definitive judgment has been pronounced. In many countries profound modifications of judicial regimes and imprisonment must be carried out in this direction. These reforms must go further and permit access to justice to all without favoring the rich in comparison with the poor. . . . Nevertheless in countries reputed to be democratic and liberal, like Belgium, France and Switzerland, for example, great reforms are still needed to attain such goals.

Finally, the effective guarantee of civil liberties is even more exacting, for it requires that in every domain the less fortunate should have the same liberty as others; a profound and methodical recasting of all the institutions of many countries is implied by such a principle, along with a rise in the standard of living for the less favored. This will reduce by just that much the necessity for the institutions' intervention on their behalf in order to guarantee their liberty.

—A severe penalty for all attacks on liberty. In the United States the Sherman Antitrust Act, the Clayton Act, and the Federal Trade Commission Act known as "antitrust law" are instructive in this regard. This legislation has severely penalized all attacks on free enterprise. Such a principle could be transposed into every domain and for all the freedoms, since where liberty is loved one cannot allow license, and one must deal severely with those who destroy liberty whether they be individuals, pressure groups, or subversive organizations.

Such a political idea must be put into effect by men whose behavior does not discredit the ideas. Degradation of morals in a society and on a political team where the finest principles of liberty are professed necessarily carries with it a degeneration of the character which renders it unsuited to the accomplishment of a great political mission. Besides, a depraved life eventually becomes common knowledge and arouses scorn.

That is why liberty cannot be validly defended except by virtuous men. It is not astonishing that the armies and regime of the Third Republic in France collapsed in a few weeks under the blows of the Nazis even though the latter were less well nourished and less numerous than their adversaries. For years alcoholism and pornography had ravaged French society from top to bottom. The awakening on May 10, 1940 was painful! And now, forty years after these sad events, the lesson is forgotten and the West tragically lacks virtue. Even in the churches where streams of purifying living water ought to be gushing forth, one sometimes hears false prophets praise license under cover of the "new morality" and perverted fundamental biblical teaching! In giving themselves over "to the bondage of sin," according to the biblical expression, Western nations risk making ready for tragic tomorrows. In losing their virtue they will also lose their liberty. Just as the Israelites had been taken captive to Babylon after having exhausted the Lord's patience because they scorned his commandments, the dissolute peoples of the twentieth century will find themselves one day, if they do not change in time, famished, naked, and lashed with blows in a sad slavery.

Requirements for the present fight for liberty

Apprenticeship in the technique of liberty is inseparable from a formation of character leading to personal mastery and a purity of life and heart which are indispensable for carrying out every great human enterprise. The conquest or conservation of civil liberty leads therefore to very great requirements on the personal level. This conquest can be accomplished only by men who have themselves obtained liberty of heart and mind, by pure men, demanding much of themselves and ready for every sacrifice.

Internal liberty is not natural to the heart of man. Although we all have a thirst for liberty, we also have within us instincts and passions which tend to enslave us. However, in the course of history there have been men who knew how to control their passions. The disciples of the Greek philosopher Zeno of Citium acquired a great renown for their austerity, their firmness in the face of every pain and testing, in a word, for their Stoicism.[1] A certain number of sages and heroes of antiquity likewise gave evidence of great virtue, especially in the original Republic of Rome. But at that time the individual was closely associated with a group where virtue was essential to honor. This collective stamp was imposed upon each person and helped to protect him from personal failures. The Japan of the Meiji provides a similar example.[2] But such virtue is contrary to liberty for it is obtained only by a constant constraint which is both individual and collective. One had to await Chrisitanity to see virtue accompanied by liberty. Again it is necessary to be specific: authentic Christianity and not its counterfeit or parody. Too often, Christ's teachings have been misunder-

---

*[1]The Greek philosopher Zeno of Citium (335-264 B.C.) founded this philosophy.

*[2]The emperor Meiji Tenno, who reigned from 1867-1926, abolished the shogunate and the feudal regime and moved the capital from Kyoto to Tokyo in 1868.

stood and "monks" under constraint have been seen to practice an ascetisim which brought nothing new compared with pagan antiquity. Christ demonstrated in his person that it was really possible to combine virtue and liberty. In everything he was entirely just and free. Up to the moment of his death, after having lived a life absolutely without sin, before the Roman governor Pilate who said to him: "Do you not know that I have authority to release you, and I have authority to crucify you?" Jesus could retain an entire internal liberty because he was resting with certainty upon the all-powerful God. He answered Pilate: "You would have no authority over me, unless it had been given you from above." Jesus had previously stated in unambiguous terms: "No one has taken it [my life] away from me, but I lay it down on my own initiative."[3]

Jesus' life was not filled with mortifications. His constant virtue was without constraint in any area. Nobody succeeded in proving him guilty of the slightest sin even though he ate and drank like everyone else without asceticism and did not hesitate to mingle with people of little esteem and loose morals in order to preach to them the good news of God's pardon and love. In this way Jesus illustrated a life liberated from the bondage of sin without being shackled by a rigid asceticism. It is such virtue and such internal liberty that modern men who are fighting for liberty must acquire for themselves first of all. This road is difficult. There are many byways which can lead one away from the goal. The only true way is that of Jesus Christ himself. His Spirit, his very life, must penetrate to the very depths of his disciples. The Bible is the guide which leads there.[4]

In all times the men of the Bible have been marvelous fighters for liberty. Think of the Beggars of the Netherlands and Belgium,[5] of the Roundheads of England,[6] of the Huguenots[7] and Camisards of France,[8] of the Mayflower Pilgrims who founded the American nation, a nation intoxicated with liberty. They knew how to be great in combat as well as in trials of all sorts. Following the heroes of the Bible who inspired them, they too

---

[3]John 10:17-18; 19:10-11.

[4]*Le Maître*, part I.

*[5]Beggars or "gueux" was the name given to those in the Netherlands who revolted against Philip II in the War of Independence (1567-73).

*[6]These followers of Oliver Cromwell (1599-1658) revolted against the arbitrary royal power of Charles I.

*[7]This name was given to the French Protestants by the Catholics as a term of derision, probably about 1560 at or near Tours.

*[8]The French Calvinists of Cévennes who fought against Louis XIV's dragoons after the Revocation of the Edict of Nantes were called Camisards because of their shirts.

conquered kingdoms, performed acts of righteousness. . . . Quenched the power of fire, escaped the edge of the sword, from weakness were made strong, became mighty in war, put foreign armies to flight. . . . others were tortured, not accepting their release, in order that they might obtain a better resurrection; and others experienced mockings and scourgings, . . . they were put to death with the sword; they went about in sheepskins, in goatskins, being destitute, afflicted, ill treated (men of whom the world was not worthy), wandering in deserts and mountains and caves and holes in the ground.[9]

The secret of their extraordinary strength of character was their internal freedom. They had been liberated from the bondage of sin through their faith in Jesus Christ who also inspired their actions.

These men, so powerful and effective in the world, renew their strength by reading the Bible daily. By it they penetrate still more the very mind of God. They allow themselves to be impregnated with the Spirit of Christ who regenerated them and gave them internal freedom. Today, wherever the Bible is read and loved, such men and women will arise anew. They will struggle against the corruption and vanity of the West. They will contribute to liberating oppressed nations after having maintained their hope. Now, as formerly, the Bible is and will remain the essential food of liberty.

The Communists know it well. That is why they pursue true Christians and prevent the publication of the Bible. For the sake of appearance they permit some churches to exist after having placed docile men at their head. As a matter of fact they teach that all religions are vestiges of the past, useless outgrowths of an outmoded social organization. To persecute Christians openly would be to recognize their vitality. The Communists use more subtle tactics. Officially they proclaim religious liberty and leave the churches open—at least some of them. These churches are shown to foreign visitors who return home satisfied, praising the tolerance of the Communists. But these visitors do not know that those responsible for the churches are under the control of the police. They have been left at their posts only after having agreed to provide a weekly report on their parishioners. They are pledged not to propagate the faith and not to make derogatory remarks against atheistic communism. Faithful Christians cannot renounce in this way the precise orders of Christ who commands them to preach the gospel to the ends of the earth in spite of every human prohibition. Along the same line, within the official churches, controlled

---

[9]Heb. 11:33-38.

and stifled by the Communists, clandestine churches are created which pursue the heroic tradition of all the persecuted Christians throughout the ages. All the police machinery of the Communist States is let loose against these clandestine churches: arbitrary arrest, torture, deportations, and much else. But it achieves no more success than did the Roman emperors or the Sun King.[10] The blood of martyrs has always been an extraordinary seed for Christians, and the gospel is being propagated today right under the noses of the leaders. Thus, a great hope arises for the enslaved peoples who see the persecuting regime being undermined from within.

The Communists' attitude toward the Bible is comparable to the one they have adopted toward the churches. Officially they claim that they do not fear it. They say that this book reflects out-of-date conceptions and that the Communist doctrines will naturally compel recognition of themselves. To save face they authorize a few limited printings of the Bible and works of translation. But, as a matter of fact, they tragically keep even the believers in the official churches from providing themselves with Bibles! The faithful copy texts into notebooks which they circulate among themselves. An effort to ''smuggle Bibles'' across the frontiers is being carried on.

There can be no question here of giving a detailed study of this extraordinary fight of the clandestine churches in the Eastern countries and of the efforts which are being made by them and by the Christians of the free world who are finally alarmed enough to distribute the Bible to these enslaved peoples. Literature about this fight began to be published a few years ago despite the wall of indifference, the blocking, and the threats which hindered it even in our countries, however democratic.[11]

This fight is the same as the one for liberty. The Communists are not deceived about this. Only the Westerners appear to forget it. They should be active in distributing the Bible in their homeland and in having it read and studied in the schools and universities and in all the homes. In a society whose fundamental principles come from the Bible, is it not strange that it is not studied more, as well by unbelievers as believers, freely and without

---

*[10]Louis XIV's passion for glory earned him this nickname.

[11]Readers who would like more details on this exciting and dramatic subject may refer to the following works: J.G.H. Hoffmann, Th.D., *Eglise du Silence* (éditions La Table Ronde); R. Wurmbrand, *Mes Prisons avec Dieu* (Tournai, Belgium: Editions Casterman); R. Wurmbrand, *L'Eglise du Silence tourturée pour le Christ* (46 rue Dufour, Paris 6ème, France: éditions Apostolat des Editions); Frère André, *Le contrebandier* (10, rue de Fribourg, Geneva, Switzerland: éditions L'Eau Vive; André Martin, *Les croyants en URSS,* éditions Fayard.

constraint? Still, what a strange silence in the school manuals, elementary curricula, and advanced studies of our countries of the Western world! Under these circumstances, why be astonished that liberty is shaky and that totalitarianism of the right or the left still remains menacing, ready to seize power with the first difficulties of an internal or international order?

We saw above that Roman Catholicism was largely responsible for the origin of this situation. For a long time it prevented the faithful from reading the Bible. Pope Pius IX, in an encyclical of December 8, 1864, described even the Bible Societies as "plagues." Consequently the countries stamped with the Catholicism of the Council of Trent methodically organized a wall of silence around the Bible. The Roman hierarchy knew very well that the spread of this extraordinary book would cause a powerful breath of liberty to pass over the entire society, which would sweep away the monarchical or dictatorial institutions which they preferred on the civil plane as well as on the ecclesiatical one.

Since the Council of Vatican II and the second Pope John XXIII, a new current has crossed the old Roman edifice. The Bible is no longer banned. The Catholics themselves are making a great effort to distribute the Bible, adding to the immense work which has been accomplished by the Protestants. Catholics throw themselves passionately into the study of the Bible which is now available at reasonable prices in new versions, formats, and even as illustrated magazines presented in the most modern manner. The Roman structure, which was formerly congealed into a great apparent unity, is now cracking everywhere. Could it be that there will come out of it a new biblical and living Church, centered on Christ, one which has regained the faith of the first Christians? The tremendous circulation of the Bible which is going on at present is certain to have an immense and far-reaching effect on the defense of liberty, provided it penetrates all areas of thought. Time will be necessary however—probably a generation—for all the wall of silence to break down in the schools and universities as well as in the thinking of Christians. Will there not be between now and then a return to persecution? Will the Roman hierarchy not try to seize the Bible again just as Pharaoh, after having liberated the Israelites from their harsh servitude, pursued them to his misfortune and that of his armies?

One must be vigilant. The fight for liberty never ceases.

Today the young States of Asia and Africa are also aware of this. They have a great deal to accomplish: to abandon the feudal or tribal structures which are no longer suitable for the problems of our time; to avoid seizure by the great powers; and to fashion for themselves in accordance with their own character a society which is just, prosperous, fraternal, and free.

Here again it is the men who count. It is important that these young nations know how to cultivate their people well so as to see rise up in their midst a generation of free men. To achieve this there is only one fundamental means: to encourage the distribution of the Bible, that food which is essential to liberty. The ruling people of these countries enjoy the privilege of having before their eyes the successful and unsuccessful experiments of the old Western States. They can ascertain the misdeeds of clericalism, of concordat regimes, as well as those of monarchical totalitarianism, fascist or Communist. They know the immense danger which a nation will run if it launches a campaign against the Bible in the form of open persecutions or simply by a wall of silence set up around it.

Will new countries have the necessary wisdom and discernment? Will they know how to be more prudent than the Europeans and build for tomorrow, in the hot regions of the globe, a happy and prosperous new world where liberty will reign?

The future of these young States is already beginning to be outlined. It is sufficient to set up the map of those where the Bible can be distributed freely. In this connection there is reason for great hope. The statistics published by the United Bible Societies on the subject of the increase in Bible distribution allow one to glimpse where there is hope of liberty in the world. Australia and Africa follow right after North America which leads in Bible distribution. Asia and South America also have significant increases. On the contrary, in Europe the statistics reveal a disquieting situation, for there biblical distribution is tending to regress.[12]

But there are lights in the night. Will this hope of liberty triumph even though immense territories and numerous populations of Europe and Asia have fallen under the totalitarian vise of regimes which lay claim to a universal empire? From the human point of view one may be pessimistic: man knows how to achieve liberty; the means are within his grasp, quite close to him; but too often, alas, he does not consider them. And the bonds of his servitude are tightened.

However the great Liberator is going to come.

Before him the most powerful empires will crumble and his reign of peace, love, justice, and liberty will be established in our world. All the oppressed, all the slaves, all the persecuted and tortured who have placed their hope in him, can therefore from this moment raise their heads and rejoice while awaiting that glorious future.

---

[12]Alliance biblique française, member of the United Bible Societies, statistics from 1971 to 1977.

And I saw heaven opened; and behold, a white horse, and he who sat upon it is called Faithful and True; and in righteousness he judges and wages war. . . . And he is clothed with a robe dipped in blood; and his name is called The Word of God. And the armies which are in heaven, clothed in fine linen, white and clean were following him on white horses. And from his mouth comes a sharp sword, so that with it he may smite the nations; and he will rule them with a rod of iron; and he treads the wine press of the fierce wrath of God, the Almighty. And on his robe and on his thigh he has a name written, "KING OF KINGS, AND LORD OF LORDS."

(Rev. 19:11, 13-16)

Christ, the glorious liberator, whom we saw suffering and crucified, is going to return as a conqueror to fulfill all his promises throughout the entire world:

The Spirit of the Lord is upon me,
Because the Lord has anointed me
To bring good news to the afflicted;
He has sent me to bind up the brokenhearted,
To proclaim the favorable year of the Lord,
And the day of vengeance of our God;

(Isa. 61:1-2)

CONCLUSION

The Tragedy of Our World

It is distressing to know that men today are dying of hunger, constantly perishing in war, or groaning in servitude. But what a tragedy to discover, as we have in each of the preceding studies, that these are not calamities for which there is no remedy. . . . The precise analysis of the problems of bread, peace, and liberty in the world has always led to the same conclusion: this evil is not inevitable. A remedy exists, one which has been tested. It is possible to build up nations which are prosperous, strong, just, free, and fraternal. But a strange blindness prevents the majority of our contemporaries and most of the leaders of States from utilizing this remedy. One would say that they prefer the ravages of famine and war and the sufferings of servitude to pledging themselves to the way that would give them bread in abundance, peace, and liberty. Reality is more complex, however. Like the French in 1936, men allow themselves to be seduced by the first sirens who come singing to them of illusory bread, peace, and liberty in order to draw them more certainly toward the rocks where they will be shipwrecked and where they will experience the opposite of their hopes and dreams.

Such a blindness, such a faculty for believing lies and setting aside the truth, such a penchant for evil, such a misunderstanding of the good, such a weakness before sirens of all sorts are only varied forms of what the Bible calls by the ancient name of "sin." It is a word which one scarcely uses in modern language. But its reality is nonetheless more evident than ever. The first and great commandment of God is: "You shall love the Lord your God with all your heart, and with all your soul, and with all your mind."[1] The greatest sin therefore is to live without loving God and without thinking of him. Is not our modern materialistic world characterized by this major sin?

---

[1] Matt. 22:37.

The same conclusion to which we were invariably led in each of the previous sections does not consist only of choosing a good political, economic, and social system. Besides, no government is perfect, although all possess valid elements. Totalitarian regimes as well as decadent democracies have a pernicious character. Profound structural reforms are indispensable, as much in the West as in the East, in order to humanize institutions and to bring about a fraternal reign with justice.

The true solution requires the presence in the city of men and women of a particular quality and animated by a certain spirit, men and women who are in some way the first fruits of a new humanity. This human quality and this spirit cannot be acquired by a mere modification of social structures as the Marxists think. An internal regeneration is necessary which only a miracle can bring about. Whoever repents of his sin and believes[2] in Jesus Christ, who died on the cross of Golgotha for the salvation of humanity and who rose again on Easter, has received this new birth. He has become a child of God.[3]

The true new humanity grows on a land sown with Bibles. All of our preceding studies have underscored this fact. Because of this any State whatsoever can very simply and at no expense receive with abundance this seed of life, without the slightest partiality, the slightest subsidy. It is enough to establish and guarantee religious liberty. Faithful Christians, true disciples of Christ, under the spiritual guidance of their leader, who is invisible to the eyes of the world,[4] will then be able to go about distributing the Bible, creating faithful churches, sowing all of society with men and women with regenerated hearts, who will be the ferment of a silent revolution bringing among other things, bread, peace, and liberty, to the greatest extent possible in our sinful world.[5]

The same moral and social renewal which occurred in England following the religious awakening which was spurred by the preaching of Wesley can be reproduced everywhere else today. However, if one were to traverse the entire world, in what States could one find this religious liberty? Here it is clericalism and State religion: Catholic, Muslim or Communist; elsewhere liberty is theoretically assured but in practice, majority pressure

---

[2]The word "believe" is employed in its strongest sense: to have faith and trust, listening with complete assent and obedience to the teaching given by Christ and reported in the Bible.

[3]John 1:12-13.

[4]John 14:19.

[5]*Le Maître,* part II, chap. 3: "The spiritual and historical foundations of the modern world."

groups are set up to take possession of the media and public instruction. What a bloody tragedy, for the consequences are there, obvious, before our eyes: sickly and poorly nourished children, sometimes starving; bodies mutilated, torn by shells and bombs; refugees, widows, orphans and all those vast regions of the world where people live permanently under the terror of arbitrary arrests!

How exact are these words from the Gospel of John:
And the light shines in the darkness; and the darkness did not comprehend it. . . . There was the true light which, coming into the world, enlightens every man. He was in the world, and the world was made through him, and the world did not know him. He came to his own and those who were his own did not receive him.

(John 1:6, 9-11)

What darkness in our world, what tragedy!
Meanwhile, let us continue our reading of the Gospel. We shall hear marvelous words of hope:
But as many as received him, to them he [that light] gave the right to become children of God, even to those who believe in His name, who were born not of blood, nor of the will of the flesh, nor of the will of man, but of God. And the Word became flesh, and dwelt among us, and we beheld his glory, glory as of the only begotten from the Father, full of grace and truth.

(John 1:12-14)

Again therefore Jesus spoke to them, saying, "I am the light of the world; he who follows me shall not walk in the darkness, but shall have the light of life."

(John 8:12)

"While you have the light, believe in the light, in order that you may become sons of light."

(John 12:36)

For twenty centuries every man has been called to choose personally between the light of Jesus Christ and the darkness of a world without God. Will he become a child of light, a child of God, that is, a man liberated from his egotism and his pride, regenerated internally by the word of God and the work of the Holy Spirit in order to glorify God and to serve his neighbor with love? Or will he continue to live according to his passions and his sinful nature without considering God? Even today men and women, young people and adults, are choosing this light, just as often in our indifferent and materialistic West as in the atheistic and Christian-persecuting East. This decision carries with it the most decisive contribution to the struggle for bread, peace, and liberty, while awaiting and preparing for the glorious return of Jesus Christ.